*Have a Good Day!*

# *Have a Good Day!*

## AND OTHER SERMONS

by

John W. Rilling

MULHENBERG PRESS     *Philadelphia*

To MARY CATHERINE

# Preface

The spectacle of sermons in print has been compared to a visit to a mortuary for the purpose of viewing a departed friend. What we cherished—the smile, the personality, even the mannerisms are all gone, leaving only the cold and lifeless remains. Granting a measure of truth to this observation, it may still be hoped that something beside remains to edify, admonish and encourage even when sermons are "laid out" in cold type.

Pascal once rebuked an author for speaking proudly and possessively of "my book." Pascal's point was that every author draws upon the stored up wisdom of the past in others' books and finds his better thoughts coming from the living encounter of mind with mind. Such dual indebtedness the present writer is only too happy to acknowledge.

But this little volume is in a more immediate sense "our book." Its substance came from the thrilling encounter of weekly worship in a congregation whose hunger for the Word of God is a constant challenge and encouragement. The suggestion that manuscripts might be turned into printer's copy came from Mrs. Orlando Berg. Despite her overcrowded secretarial schedule she found time to prepare the typescript and enlisted the willing collaboration of Miss Agnes Blank, Mrs. Ruth Blank and Mrs. Harvey Jackson in this arduous task. To each of them is due warmest gratitude for "our book."

JOHN W. RILLING

*St. John's Lutheran Church, Washburn Park*
*Minneapolis, Minnesota*
*July 12, 1958*

# CONTENTS

# HAVE A GOOD DAY!

"He that would love life and see good days, let him keep his tongue from evil and his lips from speaking guile; let him turn away from evil and do right; let him seek peace and pursue it"—I Peter 3:10-11.

IN A little book of character sketches published about two hundred years ago, William Law drew some pictures which seem remarkably up-to-date and remind us of some of our own traits. One of these characters is a young woman named Eugenia. Like most of us Eugenia has a picture of herself not as she is, but as she is some day going to be. She will be married and the mistress of a considerable household. Her house will be a school of religion, her children and servants will be brought up in the strictest practice of piety; she will spend her time, and live in a very different manner from the rest of the world.

Then the author breaks in and says, "It may be so Eugenia. You intend all this with sincerity. But you are not yet at the head of a family, and perhaps never may be. But you have now one maid, and you do not know what religion she is of. She dresses you for church, and then you go off and leave her at home to have as little Christianity as she pleases. . . . You need not stay to be that extraordinary person you intend to become; the opportunity is now in your hands, you may now live in as different a manner from the rest of the world as ever you can in any other state. Your maid is your family at present, she is under your care; be now that religious governess that you intend to be, teach

1

her the catechism, exhort her to pray, take her with you to church, persuade her to love the divine service as you love it, edify her with your conversation, fill her with your own notions of piety, and spare no pains to make her as holy and devout as yourself. When you do thus much good in your present state, then you are that extraordinary person that you intend to be; and till you thus live up to your present state, there is but little hope that the altering of your state will alter your way of life." [0]

How like Eugenia we all are. Not in having a maid, to be sure, but in having big ideas of what we are going to do or be when the conditions are favorable: The check that we would like to write some day—when economic conditions make it possible and our ship comes in; the kind of devotional life we would live if only our peculiar circumstances didn't prohibit it; the Christian attitude of forbearance and forgiveness which we would like to exhibit, if the people we have to deal with weren't quite so difficult. Yes, Eugenia, "man never is, but always to be blest." "In the sweet bye and bye," we shall do thus and so.

We shall do nothing of the sort! Our text today is of one mind with William Law. Peter is convinced that the time to "do right" is *now. This* is the day which the Lord has made. "Every day is a little life; and our whole life is but a day repeated. Those, therefore that dare lose a day are dangerously prodigal; those that dare misspend it, desperate." In a very real sense, it is now or never.

If we are to have a good day today, there are several things that Peter would remind us of. There are certain things that we must do as Christians, and certain things that we must be content to leave undone. Further, there are certain things that we must be prepared to have done to us just because we are Christians.

Our text opens with a kind of five-pronged reminder of things we must do if we are to have a good day, and the five fingers grow out of the hand of constructive helpfulness. Listen to Peter, ". . . have unity of spirit, sympathy, love of the brethren, a tender heart and a humble mind." Two forces are at work in the world; the centrifugal, which tends to alienate, to separate, to drive apart; and the centripetal, that which binds together, creates fellowship. Is there any doubt as to which is the Christian force? Listen to our Lord in his high-priestly prayer praying, " . . . that they all may be one; as thou, Father, art in me, and I in thee, that they also may be one in us . . . I in them, and thou in me, that they may be made perfect in one." It is the will of God that there be perfect unity on earth. There is no better time than the present to work for it.

Recently a half dozen of the leaders of the churches in our country went to Russia as guests of the Russian Orthodox Church. The delegation embodied in its make-up and in its composite spirit the biblical injunction to be wise as serpents and harmless as doves. Sometimes our diplomats are wise as serpents, and sometimes, we feel they are a little too harmless as doves, and have at times exhibited an unhappy faculty of losing friends and influence in world affairs. But these men, without political power, went on a peace mission, which may have far-reaching effects. The president of our church, Dr. Franklin Clark Fry with his great gifts of mind, was one of these ambassadors. There was a negro minister (his very presence might counteract certain propaganda). A famous Wall Street lawyer, who is a Christian layman of high standing, might likewise be expected to make an impression. They went not without a certain risk, and certainly with the possibility of misunderstanding by men of ill will in this country, but if the world is drawn a little closer together, if tension is lessened, then that calculated risk was well taken. They sought peace *and* pursued it.

Unity, sympathy, philanthropy with a tender heart and a humble mind, that is our job today in our own situation. I read recently an account of some men who were stationed at Hong Kong on one of our destroyers. Far from home, they learned that they were destined to spend Christmas off the coast of Greece. Feeling that the day would be far from cheerful for themselves, they decided the best way to make it a merry Christmas was to make it a little brighter day for somebody else. So one of the men wrote a letter to a Greek orphanage and asked whether they might not have thirty children as their guests on board for a Christmas party and dinner. The offer was accepted with alacrity. To get ready for Christmas, in mid-summer one of the men wrote his mother in Chicago and asked her to spend the money they had collected—some eight hundred dollars—for the biggest and best Christmas that could be provided. The store heard about it and threw in half again as much in gifts. It was a merry Christmas for thirty children such as they had never seen before. One of the men said the thing he was most concerned about was what would happen when these children returned to the orphanage. To his surprise, when they came back home, the favored children at once began to share their bounty with their less favored fellows. I am sure that when the men on that destroyer went to sleep that night, they could have echoed the sentiments of Peter, "He that would love life and see good days" let him have unity, sympathy, philanthropy, a tender heart, and a humble mind.

> Count that day lost whose low descending sun
> Sees from thy hand no deed of kindness done.

To have a good day, moreover, one must be willing not only to do these things, but to leave some other things undone. "Let him keep his tongue from evil and his lips from speaking guile." Silence, we say, is golden. God's greatest works are done in silence. So, often, are man's. Two men were visiting a great steel plant where the hammering and the din, the noise and confusion, were so great that they could hardly exchange any words, even though they stood side by side. Then, they passed into the engine room, and it was like passing from babel into silence. The power house was the quietest place in the plant. Let us take time every day to be still and say:

> Drop thy still dews of quietness,
>   Till all our strivings cease;
> Take from our souls the strain and stress,
> And let our ordered lives confess
>   The beauty of thy peace.

To have a good day we need that golden silence—where we can let our souls catch up with our bodies.

Would today be better if we talked less and listened more? That is, if we talked less with men and listened more for the voice and the will of God? Would it be any less a good day, if we left unsaid that unkind word, that carping criticism, that wounding bit of gossip? Charles Simeon of Cambridge made for himself three rules to which he adhered strictly. "1. To hear as little as possible whatever is to the prejudice of others. 2. To believe nothing of the kind until I am absolutely forced to do it. 3. Always to believe that if the other side were heard a very different version would be given of the matter. I consider love as wealth, and as I should resist a man who would come and rob my house, so would I resist a man who would weaken my regard for any human being."

It is hard not to escape the feeling that behind our epistle is some personal experience that colors the text. Peter, certainly, was made a Christian as much by the silences of our Lord, as by his words. That silent look of reproach as their eyes met momentarily in the courtyard of the high priest's palace spoke volumes. Reproach, recrimination, the unkindest cut of all: "I told you so, but you wouldn't believe me" —none of these came from the lips of the suffering servant of the Lord. If only he would have vented his spleen, Peter might have found some words to excuse himself, but that silence was devastating—and redeeming.

After Easter, when they met face to face, there was no reading of the minutes of the last meeting, with corrections and additions. Just this: "Simon, son of Jonas, lovest thou me?" That was all. But that was enough. Charity covereth a multitude of sins. Then the commission, "Feed my sheep," which included forgiveness and restoration in one. The past was swallowed up in the present call to new service.

What he did for Peter, he has done for us too. "If thou, Lord, shouldest mark iniquities, O Lord, who shall stand? But there is forgiveness with thee, that thou mayest be feared." Day by day he forgives you, day by day he makes intercession for you, day by day reconciles you unto God, or else things would be in a very bad state as far as we are concerned. As he is, so should we be. "A good day is one in which one has forgotten two things and remembered one —forgotten to complain and accuse on the one hand, and to accuse oneself on the other." It would be a good thing for us to begin each day with the words of that beautiful fifth-century morning hymn:

> No sinful word, no deed of wrong,
>     Nor thoughts that idly rove,
> But simple truth be on our tongue,
>     And in our hearts be love.

Peter's third suggestion for having a good day is this: We must be prepared to have certain things done to us. It may be very hard to take, but here it is: "Do not return evil for evil or reviling for reviling; but on the contrary bless, for to this you have been called, that you may obtain a blessing." The most natural thing in the world is to return evil for evil. You see children playing, then one pushes and the other one pushes back. The first one pushes again—because he has been pushed—only a little harder. It ends in a brawl, because no man has yet devised a way of returning tit for tat, of measuring with the same measure that it has been measured out. We are called as Christians to bless, not to curse, to reduce the tensions, not increase them.

Peter Green tells of a church leader who was called in once to referee a church squabble in which it was expected that tempers would flare and only the unregenerate would be amused and would say, "See how these Christians love one another!" He prepared himself for this grueling meeting by writing a verse from the Bible on a slip of paper.

During the meeting, when his own temper was getting the better of him, he would cool it off by referring to the paper. The disputants in the case, feeling that unfair advantage was being taken of them, demanded to see the note to which he was making such constant reference. He refused at first. Then, when they threatened to make a scene, he agreed to pass it around, if each man was permitted to read it for himself. The words they read were from our epistle: "Finally, all of you, have unity of spirit, sympathy, love of the brethren, a tender heart and a humble mind. Do not return evil for evil or reviling for reviling; but on the contrary bless, for to this you have been called." The meeting that began in rancour broke up in reconciliation. Would God that all of us—in the home, in our work, in our church, and in the world—had more skill in being lightning rods, drawing the ire of our enemies and dissipating it harmlessly by grounding it in our undiscouragable good will.

He that would love life and see good days—this is the day. "Yesterday is but a dream, tomorrow is only a vision, but today well-lived, makes every yesterday a dream of happiness, and every tomorrow a vision of hope. Look well, therefore to this day." *And have a good day today!*

# THE WONDER OF FORGIVENESS

> "Then his lord, after that he had called him, said unto him,
> O thou wicked servant, I forgave thee all that debt, because
> thou desiredst me: Shouldest not thou also have had compas-
> sion on thy fellowservant, even as I had pity on thee?"
> —Matthew 18:32-33.

ONE OF the most brilliant writers of the nineteenth century,
whose star of influence has by no means waned, was the
Russian Dostoevski. A tragic thing happened to him in his
late twenties that marked him for life, made him a writer,
and gave his life its melancholy seriousness. Like so many
people of his day, Dostoevski was vitally interested in the
social questions that were being so avidly discussed in that
age of social unrest and ferment. His interest led him to join
a society which had as its purpose such discussion. The
secret police, however, suspecting other purposes than mere
talk, raided the room where they were meeting and arrested
the members. With thirty-two others, Dostoevski was
charged with conspiracy against the czar. After a hurried
trial, they were all sentenced to death. The condemned
men discovered afterward that the sentence was a grim jest
on the part of the czar and his lieutenants, who thought by
this expedient to frighten them and give a warning to other
radical thinkers.

On a bitter morning, with the temperature many degrees
below freezing, the thirty-three were led out to the prison
courtyard, stripped of their clothing and, nearly naked,
compelled to stand half an hour while the burial service
was slowly read. Facing them stood the soldiers with their

muskets. At the very last moment, when the muskets were already aimed, a messenger rushed in waving a white flag, and announced that the czar had commuted the sentence to one to ten years' exile in Siberia. Under the strain several of the prisoners had lost their reason; several others died shortly afterward. Dostoevski passed courageously through the ordeal, but it left him ever afterward a marked man. He never could recall the experience without a shudder, and the epileptic condition which was to plague him the rest of his days had its inception that day.

I want to begin with that grim incident because I think it can help us to an understanding of our text. This is the story of the man who was forgiven a debt of astronomical dimensions, but who failed to realize that such royal forgiveness as he received obligated him to a similarly royal mode of forgiveness in his relations with others.

What a wonderful thing it was for that Russian lad to hear that the czar had commuted his sentence. Even so dubious a boon as ten years in Siberia was good news because it at least meant life instead of death, and offered the hope of freedom following the serving of his sentence. But, friends, what you and I receive from the King of kings is full pardon, full reprieve: "Then the lord was moved with compassion . . . and forgave him the debt." The good news of the gospel, the news of forgiveness, ought to be the most wonderful thing in life. The day we first heard and first understood it ought to be a red letter day of such magnitude and moment as to stand out above all others. Such has indeed been the case for some.

For Luther, for example, the quest for forgiveness was the

one thing needful, more important for him by far than the question of how to earn a living, or how to get success. It became a quest so absorbing and so all important that it became a feverish obsession. The fire in his bones was so consuming that in half an hour's time, Luther said, it would have devoured his spirit and reduced all to ashes. When, in the mercy of God, the fire was quenched, and the peace of God which passeth all understanding took possession of his heart and mind, this assurance, this pardon, was a never-to-be-forgotten experience. His whole life was altered by the wonder of forgiveness. "He hath redeemed me a lost and condemned creature . . . . in order that I might live under him in his kingdom, and serve him in everlasting righteousness, innocence, and blessedness, even as he is risen from the dead and lives and reigns to all eternity. This is most certainly true."

And it was this same experience of the wonder of forgiveness that took the burden from John Bunyan's back, and put a song upon the lips of Isaac Watts and lent wings to his words as he wrote what has been called the greatest hymn in the English tongue:

> When I survey the wondrous Cross
> On which the Prince of Glory died,
> My richest gain I count but loss,
> And pour contempt on all my pride.
>
> Were the whole realm of nature mine,
> That were a tribute far too small:
> Love so amazing, so divine,
> Demands my soul, my life, my all.

And this is the thing that troubles me—why does this central message of the New Testament not evoke a greater response in our hearts? Was Luther different from us of the twentieth century? Were Watts and Bunyan, and for that matter, Matthew, Mark, Luke, and John and Peter and Paul made of different stuff, that they could never somehow get over the wonder of forgiveness?

A visitor to this country was asked his impression of the church in America, and with blunt candor he said that there were two things that disturbed him. He noticed no moistened eyes, no trembling of the lip when we surveyed the wondrous cross, and he failed to see any trembling of hands when men reached for the cup of the Lord's Supper and heard those poignant words, "Given and shed for you for the forgiveness of sins."

Can it be that we treat forgiveness so lightly because we fail to see that forgiveness is costly—yes, costly even for God himself. When he said, "I forgive you" to the hopeless debtor (whose obligations in today's reckoning would be in the neighborhood of $17,000,000), he could not with a stroke of the pen wipe out that obligation. He assumed it himself. Forgiveness is a costly thing.

Men have always wondered whether the central Christian message of forgiveness was not immoral. Must not a man pay his own debts in the moral realm as he does in the mercantile world? The question is quick to arise, "If it is true that where sin abounds there grace much more abounds, are we to continue in sin that grace may abound?" St. Paul emphatically repudiates the suggestion, for no one who has been to Calvary can ever again take sin lightly. There, if ever, a man dies to sin and becomes a forgiven sinner, saved by grace.

If then, as the parable suggests, we can never pay God back, what then? We can, as Luther suggested, become little Christs for our neighbors. We can, indeed, *must* incarnate in our words and deeds what we have experienced of Christ. We too must learn to forgive as we have been forgiven.

"The New Testament," as John Wesley with unwearying insistence repeated, "knows nothing of solitary religion." The I-Thou relationship is implicit from the first prayers we lisp on through life. We pray, "forgive us . . . as we forgive." We can no more have forgiveness for ourselves alone on a vertical plane without the horizontal also, any more than we can possibly get an electric light to burn with only one wire connected.

It is for this reason that the New Testament insists over and over again on the importance of a forgiving spirit, one that does not harbor resentment, one that lives the beatitude, "Blessed are the peacemakers." If we are children of the Father we will expand the circumference and improve the quality of our forgiveness. Peter had just asked Jesus, "Lord, how often shall my brother sin against me, and I forgive him? As many as seven times?" What Peter really wanted to know was not how long he ought to keep on forgiving, but how soon he could stop forgiving! The rabbis had said three was a good number. Peter thought a Christian should "go the second mile" so he suggested seven. But Jesus makes it seventy times seven. In other words, as long as there is any possibility of peacemaking. In this same chapter in Matthew there are rules for the church in which the directive is given that if there are differences between believers, their obligation is to go and talk it over man to man. "If he listens to you," then, says Jesus, "you have gained your brother." If that fails, the next step is to take two witnesses, but if that fails, then tell it to the church. I have always assumed that "telling it to the church" meant giving up the attempt at reconciliation, recognizing a stone wall for a stone wall and giving up butting your head against a heartbreaking situation. But if the church is made up of those who have received the grace of God's unlimited, seventy-times-seven pardon—then the process of mediation might go on indefinitely.

Jesus here puts his finger upon a point that we need to be constantly reminded of—the trivial nature of the failures and shortcomings from which we suffer compared with the truly incalculable size of our offenses against a holy and loving Father. Someone has said, you can tell how big a man is by the size of the things it takes to get his goat. Robert Coffin the New England poet describes two sisters living in an old New England homestead. Being compelled to close off the rooms of the big house, one by one, they surrendered it to the cold. And with it,

> Their lives contracted till at last
>     Their orbit was the kitchen fire;
> They sat to think where they had cooked,
>     Empty of comment and desire.
>
> Keen ways they learned to keep their souls
>     From filling one another's need;
> They found each other's tender spots
>     And knew best how to make them bleed.

The sparrow and the robins made
   Their love each year around their gate;
Inside the house two women aged
   And sat together in their hate.

Heaven lit the apple trees
   Beyond the curbing of their well;
Inside four walls, in one small room,
   There was room enough for hell.[1]

Yes, how many homes are turned into hell by the unfor-
giving spirit that demands its $17.50 in full and forgets the
$17,000,000 debt which God has remitted—or wants to
remit, if he is only permitted to do so.

How many friendships are spoiled by the eagerness of a
third party to keep things stirred up, by saying, "Do you
know what he said about you?" Luther once pictured such
a gossip, " 'Now, I'm not telling you this to hurt you, or
with evil intent as far as he is concerned, for I really wish
him well, but . . .' See," said Luther with fine sarcasm, "See
what nice fur the kitty has! Who would ever think that hidden beneath those soft paws were such sharp claws?" The
only remedy for a spirit that would blaze in righteous in-
dignation is a loving spirit that has been to Calvary and
back, and hears from one who prayed forgiveness for his
foes, "For they know not what they do." Only then can we
become bigger and better than those small-minded folk
who like to keep things stirred up. Is this the real reason
that the wonder of God's forgiveness eludes us—that we are
so slow to forgive, so quick to anger?

In Johan Bojer's story, "The Great Hunger," a newcomer
moved into a farming community. He put up No Trespass-

ing signs on his property and kept a fierce dog to give pith and point to his surly refusal of friendship. One day, his next-door neighbor's little golden-haired girl crawled under the fence to pat the dog, but the savage beast leaped for her throat and killed her. The hostility of the neighborhood mounted to fever pitch. When the stranger went to the country store, no one spoke to him, and the clerk refused to wait on him. When spring came he could not even buy seed for his land. Then the farmer whose child was killed took seed from his own granary and sowed it in the furrows of the man who had refused friendship and had in turn been refused and rejected by the community. This deed was too much for the stranger and he asked his neighbor, "Why did you do it, you of all people, the one who really has cause to hate me?" The other answered strangely, "I did it to keep God alive." He might have quoted our Lord, "If ye do not forgive, neither will your Father which is in heaven forgive your trespasses," for "he who will not forgive another has broken the bridge over which he himself must pass"—and over which God would come to us with his supreme gift, the forgiveness of sin.

# THE SECRET OF CONTENTMENT

SOME TIME AGO, a news photographer took a picture of a group of pedestrians while they stood on a busy corner of a southern city, waiting for the traffic light to change. No one knew the picture was being taken, so the result was an interesting study of human faces. As I recall it—there was the inevitable little boy on a bicycle, with an ice cream cone in his hand, and several shoppers in animated conversation; and there was one pedestrian in a hurry, chafing with impatience for the light to change; and there was a soldier in uniform. All together the camera caught a half dozen moods—worry, impatience, animation, the vacant and pensive stare, but scarcely one face on which you would be inclined to bestow a second glance. And conspicuous by its absence was the mood expressed by that gallant soul who wrote from his prison cell to his friends in Philippi: "I have learned, in whatever state I am, to be content."

How rare it is to see in any crowd a face whose appearance is the outward and visible manifestation of an inward and spiritual serenity, a peace of mind, cheerful contentment. What is the secret of contentment? How is it attained? In these days of upheaval and tension, *can* we possess it?

In one form or another men in every generation have been seeking such satisfaction. When you think just a little about it, you discover three classic answers have been given to this quest for happiness. The first can be described in this way: Contentment is simply a problem of *addition*. What makes a man fretful and unhappy is the discrepancy

17

between what he has and what he wants. Life is a fraction in which the top figure represents what he has, the lower figure stands for what he desires. Give him what he wants, and you have solved his problem.

But actually every avenue to the heart and mind is used to increase our wants and desires. For the chemist, you may be so much water and so many assorted chemicals, but for business you are twelve different sentiments, emotions, or basic desires that can be played upon singly and in combination to increase your wants. Look at your favorite magazine, and see how many motives are appealed to: the desire to get, the desire to be like others and the desire to be different from others; the motives of envy, fear, curiosity, imitation. All these lead to one promised end: do this, or avoid that, and you will achieve satisfaction and contentment, all in ten easy payments.

Yet, we dimly suspect that contentment does not lie in the mere addition to our possessions. Canon Green said with discerning insight, "*Enough* has been defined as a little more than you have." Do our possessions ever reach the saturation point of complete satisfaction?

Jesus denied that contentment is ever to be found in this way. "A man's life consisteth not in the abundance of the things which he possesseth." And this fundamental thesis he illustrated again and again: the farmer whose barns were not big enough to hold all his goods and who said, "I will tear down my barns and build larger"; the man who was clothed in purple and fine linen, and fared sumptuously every day. But neither of these men were held up as examples for imitation. Not by simple addition of things desired does contentment come, because there is no end to the things man desires.

Leo Tolstoy has a story that he called simply "Greed." You may remember it. A Russian farmer bargained for a farm with some barbarians who apparently had no knowledge of the value of land. For a thousand rubles, they told him, he could have as much land as he could encircle on foot in one day, from sunrise to sunset. There were just two conditions. One, he was to carry a spade and dig holes at intervals, into which fence posts would be set, and his boundaries clearly marked. The other condition was that, on pain of forfeit of both money and land, he must return to the starting point by sunset of the same day.

The sun was just peeping over the eastern horizon when he started out. Eagerness lent wings to his feet. Every time he stopped to dig a hole for those who followed with posts he smiled with great satisfaction—this was his land, all his— and dirt cheap. Noon came, and he thought of stopping for rest and refreshment. But every moment lost now, would be lost forever—he could rest and eat at leisure another day. *Now* there were more important things to do.

Then the sun passed the zenith, and it was time to turn back toward the starting point. If only he had not been quite so ambitious in the morning. He ached in every bone, his breath came in racking sobs, his heart pounded like a trip-hammer. Finally he could go no farther. He staggered and fainted dead away from sheer fatigue. How long he lay there he did not know, but when consciousness returned he could see the golden ball of the setting sun still visible though rapidly sinking over the hilltop which was his starting point, and the goal he must still reach somehow. He stumbled to his feet, ran frantically up the hill, and fell a second time. This time he did not stir. He was dead. With his own spade they dug his grave and buried him. How much land does a man need beyond six feet by three? It is *not* by addition, says Tolstoy, that contentment is to be found.

The second classic answer to the secret of contentment is just the opposite of the first. A heart at peace with itself is gained by subtraction. Buddha, you may recall, asks what it is that causes unhappiness, and his answer is also unfulfilled desire. However, his suggestion is that you can find contentment only by quenching the burning fires of appetite and craving.

The same suggestion was made by another—Diogenes, the eccentric who went about with a lamp looking for an honest man. Diogenes bade his unhappy fellow countrymen to consider the simple life of the animals, a dog, for example. A dog, he said, is faithful and brave; it has no bodily shame and few wants. A dog needs no clothes, no house, no possessions. So Diogenes made it his goal in life to reduce his desires to the level of a dog—to the simplest of necessities: a blanket to cover his limbs, a bowl with which to beg his food, a staff to beat off dogs and bad men, as he said. Instead of a house he took up quarters in a wooden tub. He begged his food. He had nothing to fear from thieves, because there was nothing that anybody would want to take from him. Learn to fear nothing, desire nothing, and possess nothing, and the result will be contentment.

As a protest and a corrective Diogenes and Buddha certainly have their places. Many people would immediately begin to get a great deal more out of life in ease and satisfaction if they would learn to simplify.

But there is a point, it seems to me, where Buddha and Diogenes both fail to do justice to life. God has not made life to be lived down to, despised, and reduced to the lowest common denominator, but lived up to, and enjoyed. Genesis tells us that when God had finished the work of creation, he looked out upon all that he had made, and behold it was very good. But the Cynic and the Buddhist can't find anything good in life as such. And therein surely they are wrong. They have a kind of contempt for life. Macaulay said once quite unfairly that the Puritans forbade the none too gentle sport of bearbaiting not because it gave pain to the bear, but because it gave pleasure to the spectators. That ghastly sport should have been abolished on humanitarian grounds anyway; but there is an irreligious religiousness that doesn't enjoy its religion very much. Sir Walter Scott said that when he was a boy he was smacking his lips over a good bowl of Scotch barley soup when his father, in a grim mood, poured cold water in the broth. Soup was to be eaten, not enjoyed!

Here then are two answers: Contentment is to be had by *addition* to our desires, adding to the circumference of our satisfactions, and by *subtraction*, by simplifying, curtailing, and diluting the pleasures of life.

There is yet a third way—the Christian way. This is the way Paul describes in the fourth chapter of Philippians, which was written from prison. "Not that I complain of want; for I have learned, in whatever state I am, to be content. I know how to be abased, and I know how to abound; in any and all circumstances I have learned the secret of facing plenty and hunger, abundance and want. I can do all things in him who strengthens me." (R.S.V.)

The Christian secret of contentment is the secret of *multiplication*. Multiply abundance by Christ and you get a thankful heart that can be filled with wondering thanksgiving at the goodness of God. That was the failure of the rich man—he left God out. He did not have the grace of gratitude, so he missed the biggest thrill in life, the thrill of sharing with one less fortunate.

Multiply abasement, hunger, want, by Christ and you get the gallant spirit of contentment that can say I can do all things in him who strengtheneth me.

I do not know when I have been so stirred and moved by anything I have read in years as in reading the restrained but revealing story that Bishop Hanns Lilje tells of his imprisonment back in 1944. It was a Saturday afternoon in August, and he was in his study putting the finishing touches on the sermon he was to preach the following day in St. John's Church, Berlin. The doorbell rang violently. He went to the door. There stood two men from the Gestapo. "You're under arrest." A few hours later he found himself in a cell. He tells how it took all the courage and resolution a brave man possessed not to lose self-control when that steel door clanged shut behind him, and he flung himself upon his knees and upon the Everlasting Mercy. He tells how on that first Sunday his faith was multiplied by hearing someone whistle the melody of an old hymn. He sprang to his window and whistled back, "O for a thousand tongues to sing my great Redeemer's praise." So it went on, each answering the other with whistled hymns—a congregation of two; no, of two multiplied by One other. Those months and years in prison were experiences that this man of God would not go through again for all the wealth in the world. But they are experiences which now he would not be without either, for there he learned in his own experience the reality of the promise: "Yea, though I walk through the valley of the shadow of death, I will fear no evil: for thou are with me." "I can do all things in him who strengthens me."

Thomas Carlyle reports that when Oliver Cromwell was in his last sickness, he called for his Bible and desired an honorable and godly person there, with others present, to read to him this passage in Philippians Four. When it had been read, he said, "This Scripture did once save my life, when my eldest son died; which went as a dagger to my heart, indeed it did." Then repeating the words of the text himself, and reading the tenth and eleventh verses describing Paul's submission to the will of God in all conditions, said he, "It's true, Paul, you have learned this and attained to this measure of grace: but what shall I do? Ah, poor creature, it is a hard lesson for me to take out! I find it so!" But he read on the thirteenth verse, where Paul says, "I can do all things through Christ which strengtheneth me," then faith began to work, and his heart to find support and comfort, and he said thus to himself, "He that was Paul's Christ is my Christ too," and so drew waters out of the well of salvation.[2]

The secret of contentment—how it is to be discovered? The world says by addition. Those who hate the world say by subtraction. The Christian says by multiplication of Christ's presence and power: "I have learned, in whatever state I am, to be content." Have you not found it so too?

# WHEN LIFE LOSES ITS LUSTER

HAVE YOU ever watched a child playing by a lake or by the sea? He's been wading in the shallow water only a few minutes when he comes running to show you the beautiful stones and shells he has found. Those dripping stones are precious jewels to him. What rainbow luster in the shells he holds up for you to admire! Then, leaving his new-found treasure with you for safekeeping, he is off again for more booty. Then, you know what happens. As the stones dry, the colors fade. When he discovers it, the little fellow stands before you once more to show you the sorry remains. Those shining jewels of an hour ago are now only dull, stupid rocks. The glory has departed. It's the child's first sad experience with the vexing problem of how life can lose its luster. It will not be the last time, however, that the little fellow will be meeting this problem.

The Bible tells us the story of a man who found the luster fading from his life—Moses, the great leader of the chosen people. Paul recalls the story in the third chapter of Second Corinthians. Moses had been up on the majestic heights of Mt. Sinai for forty long days, communing with God in his deep concern over the nation he was commissioned to lead. When at last he came down the mountain to rejoin his people, he carried in his hands two precious stones, the sacred tablets, with the Ten Commandments carved upon them. But it was not the recollection of what Moses had in his hands that fascinated Paul. It was the glow on his face. Abraham Lincoln said that after a man is forty he is re-

24

•

sponsible for the way his face looks. Well, here was a man twice forty whose face was positively aglow. There was such a divine splendor upon it that the Israelites could not stand to gaze directly at him. Here was a man who had so entered into the secret place of the Most High, that his countenance shone with divine radiance. But . . . the light began to fail. Like the setting sun, fading so slowly that the eye fails to note its decline, the light faded from his brow. When Moses became aware of what was happening, he put a veil over his face, so that the Israelites might not see the end of the fading splendor.

Now, how does life lose its luster today? Well, here is a young couple, standing before the altar of their church to pledge their undying love and abiding faithfulness to each other. Their faces are positively aglow as they exchange their vows. If only they could keep the light of such love shining undimmed, through the years. Perhaps it can't be done. Perhaps God doesn't intend that the flame of romantic love should burn all through life with an incandescent glow. But surely family life was never meant to bog down into the prosaic, matter-of-fact existence through which multitudes of families muddle week after week. Can you keep family life from losing its luster?

Or, here is a person in the middle years of life who finds his work is losing the appeal it once had for him. It's a grind now, whereas it used to be a glorious affair. Now it's just a chore to be done, with the day's high point— quitting time! While I was calling upon a patient in a hospital not long ago, a young student nurse entered the room. She saw me standing at the bedside and, realizing there was no chair, volunteered to get one. While she was gone the patient told me that she had had a good many nurses during her long illness. It seemed to her that while the years added particular skills, they seemed to subtract a certain something from the spirit. The initial zest and eagerness she noted in the probationers had faded from the faces of the old-timers. How can you keep your profession from fading into a mere job?

Perhaps you have had this thing we are talking about happen in your religious life and experience too. You can look back to a time when your spiritual life was gay and triumphant; when prayer was a privilege; and when service, no matter what kind, was a delight. You were glad when they said to you, "Let us go into the house of the Lord." Against temptation, your strength was as the strength of ten, because your heart was pure. Against the selfish interests that entrench themselves behind privilege, it seemed not at all impossible to win a victory that would make the kingdoms of the world the kingdom of our Lord and his Christ. But now! You wonder if there's any use. It seems that as things have been so they remain—world without end!

Or, it may be that life has lost its luster not in this area or that, but *as a whole* life itself seems to be the thing whose worth you now question. Mark Twain was a man who enjoyed life hugely. With his zest for living, what a fascinating tale he told of *Life on the Mississippi* and elsewhere. The people that throng his books from *Tom Sawyer* to the *Innocents Abroad* all found life very good indeed. His humor is delightful as it is wholesome. Then, for Mark Twain too, the light began to fade. You can scarcely believe that the author of *The Adventures of Tom Sawyer* is the same man who wrote the following bitter summary of the meaning of life: "A myriad of men are born; they labor and sweat and struggle for bread; they squabble and scold and fight; they scramble for little mean advantages over each other; age creeps upon them; infirmities follow; shames and humiliations bring down their prides and their vanities; those they love are taken from them and the joy of life is turned to aching grief. They vanish from a world which will lament them for a day, and forget them—forever."[3] To feel like that about life, as Mark Twain did in retrospect, is surely high tragedy.

Now what can we do about this mood of disillusionment that descends like a pall over life? I suppose we do instinctively what the Scripture tells us Moses did when he discovered the luster was fading away. He tried to cover up. He put on a veil—a front, as we would say. Yet as we look into the mirror one day we discover what we don't like to see, so we pretend that it just isn't there. It may be noble pretence as in the following poem but it is still pretence:

> Though I am beaten
>   Nobody shall know.
> I'll wear defeat proudly;
>   I shall go
>
> About my business
>   As I did before.
> Only when I have safely
>   Closed the door

Against friends and the rest
  Shall I be free
To bow my head
  Where there is none to see

Tonight I will shed my tears;
  Tomorrow when
I talk with you
  I will be gay again.

Though I am beaten
  Nobody shall guess
For I will walk
  As though I knew success.

But keeping things to ourselves like that only worsens matters. Hugging misery to our breast only makes misery feel like taking off his hat and staying awhile. To cover up is no solution at all. It will all *have* to come out some day.

I wonder whether we can't find some help in meeting our problem by retracing our steps to the very place where the luster first began to fade. In Moses' case it's not hard to find. It's the place where his dreams came face to face with what we like to call "cold facts." It was when he came down from the mountain top to try to put a foundation under his dreams that Moses became disillusioned. The only freedom his people seemed to be interested in was freedom *from restraint* rather than freedom *for responsibility*. That golden calf intrigued them much more as an object of worship than the holy God whose commandments Moses brought down to them from the mountain. Like a good many of us today, they could get a great deal more excited about having a good time than about *being* good. It sounds as modern as today's paper.

Someone has said the only way not to be disillusioned is to have no illusions. And that's right. But, that doesn't mean nodding your head sagely and saying, "Well, you just can't change people." The truth is that you can't change people by just passing laws. (We should know *that* by now!) You can't regulate, legislate, or educate people into the kind of a life that they should be living. We pass laws, and wonder why people don't behave themselves. We tighten up regulations and wonder why nothing happens. We make new treaties and promise never again to go to war and wonder why we still do. People are not regulated into the abundant life; they can only be redeemed into it. Even Moses seemed to forget that when it came to the Ten Commandments. They don't begin with a prohibition, "Thou shalt *not!*" but with a promise: "I am the Lord thy God, which have brought thee up out of the land of Egypt, out of the house of bondage." When a man begins to realize all that God and others have done for him, the desire for goodness begins to blossom like flowers under the warm touch of the spring sun. You can't make people good, but you can perhaps love them enough so that gratitude will flower in goodness.

That was a thing even Moses had to learn. He never came nearer realizing his high and holy dream for his people than on that day when he stood between them and the just wrath of a holy God. He saw that Hand, poised, as he felt, about to wipe the slate clean. Then Moses offered himself as a substitute. "Oh, this people have sinned a great sin, and have made them gods of gold. Yet now, if thou wilt forgive their sin—; and if not, blot me, I pray thee, out of thy book which thou hast written." You couldn't turn your back upon a man who offered to die in order that you might have another chance to live!

Well, if you find then that life is losing its luster, try going back to the place where the light first began to fade. See if your disillusionment doesn't also come from some illusion that you should never have cherished in the first place.

Our other word of counsel suggested by the experience of Moses is this: that we not only seek the source of our disillusionment, but also return to the place where the light first began to *shine* for us. You know, it is said that the pearls of the House of Hapsburg were found one day to be losing the luster which had made them once so famous. An authority made this suggestion: Put the pearls back for a season into the very ocean depths from which they had first been taken. This was done, and the luster was restored!

If the world is not to be too much *for* us, we must see to it somehow that it is not too much *with* us. We too need to be plunged into the source of all light, of all life and truth and beauty. We need to pray with the psalmist, "Restore unto me the joy of thy salvation." For our own work we need to pray, "Establish thou the work of our hands upon us; yea, the work of our hands establish thou it." We need to experience what King David knew, and Mark Twain didn't: *"He restoreth my soul."* Like Moses, we need to ascend the hill of the Lord and regain our perspective upon life.

That's what Christ can do for you too, because he has

been doing it for countless souls down the years. Listen to Paul who had every reason to be sour on life but wasn't because of what this Christ had done and continued to do for him: "Therefore seeing we have this ministry, as we have received mercy, we faint not. . . . We are troubled on every side yet not distressed; we are perplexed, but not in despair; persecuted, but not forsaken; cast down, but not destroyed. . . . For God, who commanded the light to shine out of darkness, hath shined in our hearts, to give the light of the knowledge of the glory of God in the face of Jesus Christ." In Christ he had found the secret of keeping life's luster undimmed. His life was plunged daily in the source of joy and strength and courage.

In Germany—that land so recently darkened by tragedy— one of the bright spots you'll find is the place where the deaconesses are at work. Those present-day Good Samaritans who serve wherever there is need, without pay, are like angels without wings. But they have to be able to take it. Before the church commissions these servants it must make sure that they understand very clearly all that is involved. Each sister must answer these three questions: "Whom do you serve?" Her answer is, "I serve my Lord in his wretched ones." "What is your reward for serving?" "I do not serve for reward," comes the answer. "My reward is that I am permitted to serve." "But what of the dangers, what if you should die while serving?" "If I die, I die!" These devoted souls have found the secret of keeping the luster in life—even in life at its worst. He does it for them. He can do it for us *if* we'll only let him.

# HEAR YE! HEAR YE!

"And he took him aside from the multitude, and put his fingers into his ears, and he spit, and touched his tongue; and looking up to heaven, he sighed, and saith unto him Ephphatha, that is, Be opened"—Mark 7:33-34.

WE ARE told that those who beheld this miracle of healing and restoration were astonished beyond measure. And wherever they went they reported the good news, "He hath done all things well: he maketh both the deaf to hear, and the dumb to speak." Is "astonishment" the right word for us as we think of this miracle? Not "dubious," certainly. The miracle itself can't be questioned. Given a compassionate heart like Christ's, given a mountain-moving faith like his, given the strong fellowship with God that he enjoyed—and it would be a "miracle" if no miracle took place in such a plight as was brought to his attention. But if we aren't dubious—is "wistful" the right word for our attitude? That happened so long ago, and miracles, you know, don't happen any more.

But Luther, for one, would not agree with that attitude of mind. Indeed, he puts it the other way, "This miracle," he protests, "is really a *mere trifle*, when one compares it with the one that God performs every day. Babies are born every day who have neither hearing nor speech, and the like, yea, not even a soul or the power of reasoning—and within the space of a year it is all given to them—soul, body, speech and the like." Luther's point is that we are surrounded by miracles. What is so ordinary about this

32

wonderful thing sight—whereby the outside world is flashed through the camera of the eye upon the invisible screen of my consciousness? What is so prosaic about the process whereby a column of air passing through my vocal chords and projected from my mouth should reach your ears and there be transubstantiated by a miracle into meaning? Luther says it much more simply and directly, and with the intent that we be led to gratitude and worship of so good and so great a God. "I believe that God has made me and all that exists; that he has given and still preserves to me my body and soul, my eyes and ears, my reason and all the powers of my mind."

But have you ever wondered why Jesus performed miracles at all? Was it his sheer humanitarian spirit that couldn't stand to see suffering or privation unrelieved wherever he could help? Doubtless kindness was a part of it, but not the whole. Chiefly, his interest was not physical but spiritual. He wanted to restore not hearing alone but a relationship with God that deafness had impaired. Was that why Jesus sighed that deep agonizing sigh as he put his fingers into the man's ears to open that door long closed? He knew that ears made to hear the good, the true, the beautiful, are often contaminated with the poison of gossip or filled with the twaddle of empty talk.

You and I today have a solemn responsibility to listen for what God is saying in the midst of the world's clamor. How can it be that we who hear well enough (as far as our physical faculties go) are no better off than was the man who couldn't hear the voice of God until Christ touched him?

Recently I heard a man say with a wry smile, but with

deadly seriousness, "I am amazed at the number of so-called Christian people who are not church-broken." To illustrate his point he cited the following incident: At the inauguration of a new dean at one of the great seminaries in our country, two *ministers*, ignoring the purpose for which the congregation had gathered, and oblivious of where they were, in the midst of that solemn service carried on so animated a conversation that a woman had to ask them to be still so she could hear what the speaker down front was saying! "He that hath ears to hear, let him hear."

Long ago the Apostle Paul, writing to Timothy, was concerned that he might know "how thou oughtest to behave thyself in the house of God, which is the church of the living God, the pillar and ground of the truth." Well, do we know how we ought to behave ourselves in the house of God? Unless we know why we are here, no outward behaviour, no liturgical decorum can be of any real meaning.

Why do we gather together as a congregation? Why do we sing? Why do we read the Bible? Why do we pray? Why do we preach? Why do we have the whole context of the service? Is it not for this simple reason—that Christ may say to us, "Ephphatha—be opened"? The essence of our service, as Evelyn Underhill unforgettably phrased it, is: "God's merciful word coming to man." It's the only way that he can deal with us as persons. The law of gravity works regardless of whether the individual is a man or a mouse—but only in his Word can he deal with us as persons. God made lids for eyes, that we may close them, but none for ears, because he desires personal response to his approach to us through the Word.

The figure of Moses who came down from the mountain of God and knew not that his face shone is both illustration and inspiration. He knew why he was going to Mt. Sinai—to get some word of God for his people. He got more than a word. He got the inspiration from those forty days that illuminated his whole life. The shining countenance was but the outward and visible manifestation of the inward and spiritual grace. In worship we come to hear the Word where our experience is something like listening to a radio that must be plugged in and turned on before we can hear.

A second reason for poor receptivity might be stated in terms of the radio also. If worship is the conscious attempt to hear God's Word, a further reason for poor receptivity is that of preoccupation. If the vacuum sweeper is running in the next room, even the best radio program in the world will not come through. If the mind is already filled with its own cares and concerns, even the Lord God himself cannot make himself heard. Here in church, for example, sits a woman. Apparently she is listening to the sermon, she sings the hymns and she bows her head during prayers. But her mind is a warring confusion of voices, as she wonders whether she can go on maintaining the pretense of home life where all affection and even respect is gone. She wants advice, but she is not yet ready to cry out, "Lord, what wilt thou have me to do?" It would be a miracle, indeed, if God's Word could penetrate that soundproof barrier of preoccupation.

Tennyson tells us of the "Northern Farmer" on his deathbed. He had never failed to go to church, but there too his mind was always pre-empted by thoughts of the farm. He was physically present, but spiritually preoccupied.

An' I hallus coom'd to's choorch afoor moy Sally wur
   dead,
An' 'eard 'um a bummin' awaay loike a buzzard-clock
   ower my 'ead,
An' I niver knaw'd whot a mean'd but I thowt a 'ad
   summat to saay,
An' I thowt a said what a owt to 'a said, an I coomed
   awaay.

Jesus said that it was preoccupation with material things,
the cares of the world and the deceitfulness of riches, that
drowned out the voice of God. A wise man observed that
when a man set out to serve God and mammon, he soon
discovered that there was no God. It's the deadly peril of
preoccupation.

There is the familiar story set in New York City. Two
men were walking down one of those concrete canyons
some call streets, when suddenly one of them stopped and
laid his hand upon his companion's arm. "Listen," said he.
And, there, sure enough, far from his native haunts, was
heard the cheerful chirping of a cricket. No one else apparently heard it. The crowds surged through the streets,
intent on their business. Then, drawing a silver coin from
his pocket, the first man let it drop to the sidewalk. Immediately as though they had been set in pivots, a dozen
heads turned around inquiringly.

A penny held too close to the eye can shut out the sun.
A nickel held too close to the ear can exclude the sound of
God's voice. To what wave length are you tuned? Why
did Samuel hear the voice of God, and Eli did not? Eli
dwelt physically in the temple of the Lord at Shiloh, but
his mind was out there in the far country with his prodigal

sons. How true it is that the message fails to reach us, because our minds by preoccupation are tuned to another wave length than the one God is using.

Yet another reason for poor hearing suggests itself. It may be that we hear very well what the Lord's will is, but it's not what we want to hear. Like the sagacious colored man who was finally persuaded by his friends to see a doctor. When the doctor had examined him and written out the prescription, the patient thanked the doctor, and started out the door, when the doctor said, "That will be $2.00 for the prescription." "No suh, doctor," came the reply—"I ain't a-goin to take it." Jonah heard the Lord saying to him, "Arise, go to Nineveh, that great city, and cry against it; for their wickedness is come up before me." But instead of heading east to Ninevah, Jonah took the first boat for Tarshish and points west. He knew very well indeed what it was God was saying, but like a child that pretends not to hear, he paid no attention because he didn't intend to follow the prescription. God had to touch that recalcitrant prophet in no gentle fashion before he would obey. We are, in our generation, the children of Jonah. To be treated as roughly as our world has been with two wars in one generation—what can that be but God saying over and over again, "Ephphatha!"

Today then, as we gather for worship, we pray that He who opened the ears of the deaf may enable us to hear God's voice speaking in and to and through the events of today. And also, like the prophet who came to the temple to inquire of the Lord in a day of confusion and perplexity, let us expect to hear a Voice that still asks: "Whom shall I send, and who will go for us?" Will we answer as Isaiah did, "Here I am! Send me!"?

# WHAT CHRIST SAW IN CHURCH

"And Jesus sat over against the treasury, and beheld how the people cast money into the treasury: and many that were rich cast in much. And there came a certain poor widow, and she threw in two mites, which make a farthing. And he called unto him his disciples, and saith unto them, Verily I say unto you, That this poor widow hath cast more in, than all they which have cast into the treasury: For all they did cast in of their abundance; but she of her want did cast in all that she had, even all her living"—Mark 12:41–44.

ONE OF the most popular columns in the *Cleveland Press*, through the years, has been a weekly article called, "A Stranger Goes to Church." It is the custom of the religious editor of the *Press* to drop in, unannounced, on some church service, and to report his impressions in his next day's column.

I can still remember the Saturday night when the phone rang and the voice on the other end said, "This is Frank Stewart of the *Press*. I'm planning to attend your service tomorrow. I don't usually let people know I'm coming, but since I want to leave town early tomorrow afternoon, I'm calling to get a few advance facts."

To think of it! Frank Stewart in our little church the next day! The weather was bad . . . what would the attendance be? What would he think of the sermon? Would he think it good enough? What would he find to quote? What if nobody recognized him, ignored him, and treated him like a stranger?

An honest confession is good for the soul so I suppose

I ought to confess that I took advantage of my advance information and did all in my power to see that there was a better-than-average congregation, and that at least a half-dozen people were on the look-out for a certain stranger in church. I'm afraid the sermon suffered from my self-consciousness that day.

It seems a little foolish to get so excited just because a newspaper man was coming to church to do a column about your service. But what if another Stranger were in church today, the One Mark tells us about? Wouldn't your heart skip a beat *too*, if you suddenly, somehow, became aware that the person sitting beside you, sharing your book, listening to the sermon, handing the offering plate on to you, was none other than Christ himself?

It is instructive to remember that every service Christ attended was a service in which something strange, exciting, wonderful happened. At the very first service he attended, as a mere babe, he was brought to the temple and placed in the arms of the aged Simeon, who had been waiting for the consolation of Israel. Looking into that infant face Simeon saw a dawning glory that dimmed the light of the sun, saw the fullness of the revelation that was to be, felt sunset turn into sunrise, death into life, and cried out, "Lord, now lettest thou thy servant depart in peace . . . for mine eyes have seen thy salvation." On another occasion when he was in church, they asked him to read the scriptures. The result of *that* was a near riot, for he disturbed the worshipers' complacency, shocked them, and challenged not only their old racial pride but their treasured religious prejudices and unwarranted assumptions as well.

Today's text calls our attention to still another service

which our Lord attended, in the temple at Jerusalem. What did he see in church? Deliberately, he seated himself opposite the temple treasury. Good manners in church ordinarily suggest that you don't watch what the person next to you puts in the offering plate. But Jesus sat precisely where he *could* watch the multitude putting their offerings in the trumpet-shaped receptacles which were placed there for the upkeep of the temple and the relief of the poor.

What was it that Christ saw in church that day? Mark tells us in the verses that precede our text that He saw the people who wanted to play both ends against the middle. These were the scribes who wanted above everything else to appear religious, who loved the ceremonial robes and the salutations of the street corner, and who for a pretense made long prayers—but, Jesus noticed—also devoured widow's houses. Tainted money they put into the offering—tainted with dishonesty and stained with the blood of the oppressed. "Filthy lucre" in very fact.

We have a saying, "Money talks." I wonder sometimes what the money would say if it could really speak out when it is placed on the altar. Is there still blood money? Sharp-practice money? Or money that is "wages" for work that never has been done? What would Christ say if he came to our church today and sat where he could watch as our gifts are given?

Again Mark tells us He saw how the rich cast in much. Sometimes I think that we are less than fair to the people of means in the church. True, there are some people who are blessed above the average and they intend to keep what they have. Sudden affluence, a windfall, a bequest makes them cautious, conservative, and fearful lest they lose what they have. But there are *others* who, having been blessed with more of this world's goods, are generous supporters of every good cause.

I have just started reading the story of the life of John D. Rockefeller, one of the world's richest men, but also one of the world's most generous. As a youth of sixteen he tramped the streets of Cleveland looking for work and finally found a job that paid $3.50—not for an hour but a whole week's work. But already in that same year Rockefeller began a ledger of donations, the month of November showing contributions of $2. Not bad for a boy of sixteen— $.50 a week out of the week's $3.50. Before he was twenty-one he had given $72.22 in one year. As a young man of twenty-five his gifts swelled to $671.86, and the next year they went above the thousand dollar mark. "He had not waited to become rich before he became generous." "The rich cast in much" says Mark, and our Lord's silence as he watches, is certainly not the silence of disapproval. To whom much is given, much shall also be required.

But, then came the widow, twice afflicted—deprived of a bread winner, and poverty-stricken as well. In her hand she held two copper coins which make a penny, and into the treasury went both coins. She could have kept one for herself. Christ's verdict was that she had given *more* than all the rest. "For they all contributed out of their abundance; but she out of her poverty has put in everything she had, her whole living." (R.S.V.)

Brethren, if Jesus Christ is the same yesterday, today and forever, we can't keep this story back there in the first century and across the ocean in Palestine. If his Spirit is not present, if his eyes do not rest upon us, then what we are doing is not worship, but introspection. But God himself *is* present. He sees us. He is the stranger in our midst. So this gospel is not only about the Temple at Jerusalem, but about his temple here. He sat down opposite the treasury and he sits there today; he watched then and he watches us now in our worship and in that act of worship we call the offering. The old version reads "He beheld how the multitude cast money into the treasury." The *how* is very important. It is as important as the how *much*. The giving that passed without comment was the giving that came from the overflow. Most of our giving is out of our surplus, it is giving that we wouldn't miss anyhow.

How often a mission has reached the point of critical and desperate need, when gifts of money, food, medicines, and clothing come just as they are about to despair, and give them the lift they need to go on under their own power. But really isn't that mostly surplus giving? Clothing that we had outworn, or the children had outgrown? Is it really a sacrifice? Do we take any food out of our own mouths, or clothing off our backs? Let us not depreciate the value or the blessing of this giving. After all, he who judges is the Lord. Yet I am sure that he would say that the same holds true today as it did then—they gave of their abundance.

There is a familiar Indian legend which tells of a beggar who stood at the roadside begging with his wooden almsbowl. He had accumulated a little store, a few handfuls of rice and corn, when, looking down the road he saw the king's chariot approaching. His heart leaped up at the prospect, for the king would surely give a needy beggar a king's magnificent gift. To the beggar's astonishment, when the chariot came to where he was, the king stopped the chariot but instead of giving alms, held out *his* hand for a gift. What a royal jest—to ask alms of a begger? But the king continued to stand there with hands expectantly outstretched. He could not refuse the king, so the beggar took from his bowl a single grain of golden corn and put it in the king's hand. When he emptied out his bowl at nightfall the beggar was surprised to find one tiny nugget of pure gold just the size of the grain he had given the king. "Then," confessed the beggar, "I wept and wished that I had had the heart to give thee all." When you and I look the King in the face at last, at the end of the day, I suspect that there may be tears of regret in our eyes for a similar reason—we gave only of our abundance.

What a contrast that other gift was, if we measure it not by the amount that was put in but by the amount that was left over after the gift was given. By that measure Jesus was right in saying that she had put in more than all the rest. We sometimes speak of sacrificial giving, but most of our giving is not sacrificial in the sense that it costs us dearly. Our gifts to the Red Cross, the Community Chest, the never-ending procession of door-to-door solicitations don't cut us to the quick like the widow's contribution did. When she gave her own living it meant that she had to miss her next meal. No wonder Jesus paid her tribute of high praise. Those two coins, the smallest in circulation at that time, have paid incalculable dividends in provoking others to love and good works ever since. Anyone else standing beside Jesus that day, who happened to notice the two coins as they fell into the offering, might well have thought this amounts to very little. Had he known the circumstances he might have protested that the gift was too much, on the grounds that she certainly could not afford to give anything. Yet our Lord not only did not forbid the sacrificial gift, he commended it. For he saw, what we sometimes fail to see, that when people are no longer expected to sacrifice for a great and worthy cause, the cause is doomed. A church without an altar is no church but a hall or an auditorium. Christianity without a cross is a counterfeit. Religion without sacrifice is not religion at all, but mere philosophy.

It is interesting and instructive to remember that the place where Jesus stood that day in the temple, as he watched the giving of gifts, was not always holy ground. Once it had been secular. In the days of David, when plague was decimating the land, the word of the Lord came to the king that if he would build an altar to the Lord on Ornan's threshing floor, the plague would be stayed. David approaches Ornan as he is about the task of threshing his grain, and without any preliminaries asks for the site that he may erect an altar there. Prudently he offers a fair price. But Ornan with equal un-Oriental directness refuses to bargain, and offers it as a gift instead. "Take it; and let my lord the king do what seems good to him; see, I give the oxen for burnt offerings, and the threshing sledges for the wood, and the wheat for a cereal offering." He, in his day, was doing what the widow did in hers—making a total gift, his very living, and withholding nothing. But David demurs. "I will not take for the Lord what is yours, nor offer burnt offerings which cost me nothing." So David paid a princely price, six hundred shekels of gold for the site. And there he built an altar.

Is it any wonder that this place became hallowed ground?

Here in coming days Solomon built his temple. Here too
Jesus stood on holy ground hallowed by sacrifice, observ-
ing the multitude, how they gave.

What shall we do with this story of the widow's mite?
We can say all sorts of things, we can raise all manner of
"ifs," "ands," and "buts." We can plead our prior responsi-
bilities and obligations and evade the thrust of the story.
Or we can learn from it to mark our giving with the sign
of the cross, and find to our amazement how much the
Lord loves a cheerful giver.

> Laid on thine altar, O my Lord divine,
>     Accept this gift today, for Jesus' sake;
> I have no jewels to adorn Thy shrine
>     No farfamed sacrifice to make.
> But here, within my trembling hand I bring
>     This will of mine, a thing that seemeth small,
> But Thou alone, O Lord, can'st understand
>     How, when I yield Thee this, I yield mine all.[4]

# HOPE'S SHINING RAY

"For we know that the whole creation groaneth and travaileth in pain together until now. And not only they, but ourselves also, which have the firstfruits of the Spirit, even we ourselves groan within ourselves, waiting for the adoption, to wit, the redemption of our body"—Romans 8:22-23.

IN HIS rhapsody on love in First Corinthians 13, St. Paul concludes, "So faith, hope, love abide, these three; but the greatest of these is love." (R.S.V.) It is not hard to discover why love is greatest, because it lasts the longest of the three cardinal virtues. A day will come when we shall need neither faith nor hope. What need for faith when we shall have sight? When we shall see Him face to face, faith will have done its work. And hope too will be superfluous when hope is no more deferred. But until then, we shall need both faith and hope. Since that is so, it is strange that hope is the most slighted of the qualities of Christian living. It is neglected in our thinking, our preaching, our worship.

How often you have heard sermons on faith. We like to sing "My faith looks up to Thee." We read about it every time we open the New Testament. The entire eleventh chapter of Hebrews is devoted to faith with its thrilling roll call of the heroes of faith—Abraham and Moses and all the rest. Faith is not neglected.

How often love is our theme. A famous Scottish preacher was quizzed once, "Have you ever preached on John 3:16?"

"Nay, nay" came the reply. "It's in every sermon I preach." So it is, we trust, in ours. So it is in many of the songs we like to sing. Two of our most loved hymns speak of "the love of God," which is "broader than the measure of man's mind," and of a "love that wilt not let me go."

In contrast to that, how seldom we strike the note of hope! Is it because we are really this-worldly? Do we find ourselves so much taken up with this world which is so much with us, getting and spending, that we have little time or interest in another?

A great historian said once that he had learned four lessons from his lifelong study of history. One of those four lessons was—when it gets dark enough, you can see the stars. If we have never seen those stars, is it because we have never really felt hopeless? Have we pinned our hopes on man's contriving rather than upon that new world wherein dwelleth righteousness? Multitudes of people, if they were honest, would say that their creed is really the twenty-third Psalm revised and brought up to date in words something like this: "Science is my shepherd I shall not want. Technology maketh me to lie down in green pastures, and the science of geriatrics restoreth my soul; surely progress and prosperity will follow me all the days of my life, and I will dwell in Utopia forever." In such a case, hope may well drop out of our vocabulary, because we shall have no real need for it.

Christian hope is predicated upon the belief that progress will never bring us to the point where God has nothing left to do. The possibilities of development, the advances of science, the victories of technology, the conquests of education will never be the answer to the prayer, "Thy kingdom come, thy will be done." Christian hope is not despair of this world so much as it is a firm conviction that this world will never be able completely to satisfy our needs and desires. Like Cleopatra, we have, each of us, "immortal longings." "Hope," writes Dean Inge, "is the temper natural to the immortal spirits under temporary probation who know that God loves them, that Christ has redeemed them, and that the Holy Spirit is with them to help their infirmities," and consequently "a day is coming when the last clinging relic of a material world's power to dim the vision and interrupt the harmony of spirit and sanctity will be blown away on the winds of death, and when the last veil of weak mortality hiding the ultimate mystery will be rent in twain by God's own hands from top to bottom . . . So will we ever be with the Lord." That is the Christian hope.

In our scripture today, which is part of some of Paul's most eloquent words, the eighth chapter of Romans, Paul looks with eyes wide open into some of the dark corners of the world of nature, of human existence, and of his own soul. In that darkness he sees the stars of hope shining clear and bright. Hope sends a shining ray into nature's dark enigma. It illumines the age-old mystery of evil and suffering. It shines in the human heart with the promise that the day will dawn and the darkness flee away when God's light shines in all its fulness.

Let us look at each of these three areas in turn.

First, hope sends a shining ray into nature's dark enigma. When you read the Gospels, you find that our Lord saw in nature that which was a challenge to believe and trust. He saw the sparrow on the housetop. His eye noted how the lily of the field grew, neither toiling nor spinning, neither fretting nor worrying. Creature of a day, it trusted in God who clothes the grass and cares for all his creatures. The sower, going forth to sow and casting his seed upon the ground, is the sublime preacher of faith.

Paul does not deny this but he is aware of something else. He did not hear nature singing, he heard it sighing. His ear was attuned not to its harmony, but its discord.

It is not that Jesus is right and Paul wrong, or Paul right and Jesus mistaken. Nature is God's, and therefore good. God said so when he finished the work of creation. But Paul also knew that harmony was disturbed by the sin of man. Nature is under a curse. Having drunk the blood of Abel, the mark of Cain is upon nature. Nature has become "red in tooth and claw." The cry of the hare caught in the cruel talons of the hawk is as real as the carefree song of the lark. The whole of nature groans in a common travail all the while. But this cry is a cry of hope, of expectation. In this agonizing travail Paul senses the birthpangs of a new age for which nature waits and hopes and prays, when both nature and human nature will be restored to the paradise which has been lost.

The poet Thomas Hardy tells of walking home late one bitter winter afternoon, his heart full of those somber thoughts that coiled like a serpent about his cynical and unbelieving heart. He thought he was all alone; but suddenly overhead, a little bird, the darkling thrush, chose that moment to fling his soul in song upon the growing gloom. As far as the poet could see there was nothing to sing about in that bleak wintry scene. For a brief moment Hardy began to doubt his doubts. Could it be that in this tiny creature's breast there burned a divine hope not apparent to a doubting Thomas like himself?[5]

This is the hope of which Paul speaks in our text. Nature will share with human nature the restoration of all things which is in store for both. The Bible does not look for heaven as an abode of disembodied spirits; it looks for a new heaven and a new earth, it looks for the adoption of sons, the redemption of our bodies, of a state of peace when the lion and the lamb shall lie down together, and—in the vision of the prophet—"they shall not hurt nor destroy in all my holy mountain; for the earth shall be full of the knowledge of the Lord, as the waters cover the sea."

Our second point is that to be is to suffer. We can see suffering everywhere in nature. To be a human being also means suffering. But the Christian sees suffering in a new light, the light of hope.

Each of the religions of the world has tried to come to terms with the fact and meaning of suffering. Hinduism answers the problem by saying that suffering is retribution for evil done in a past existence. Buddhism sees it as the problem of problems and prescribes the quenching of desire as the way to stop the endlessly turning wheel of existence which means suffering. Mohammedanism, with its doctrine of God as absolute will, sees suffering as one's fate against which it is vain to rebel, and counsels submission and apathy. In our Lord's day, Hellenism tried to ignore the problem. It said that God could not suffer, and accordingly taught the impassibility of God. Hellenism drew the great spiritual leaders in such a way as to suggest that they were not amenable to pain.

Christianity comes to grips with the problem of suffering

not by denying its reality, or by positing evil as retribution for evil in some past existence, but by showing God in Christ wrestling with the powers of darkness and evil, and overcoming them. T. R. Glover finely says that men have always felt that Jesus knew "where the problems hurt." In his parables how many of the characters that appear there are real people who had felt the gnawing pangs of hunger, who knew what it meant to lie by the roadside beaten and robbed, who had stood idly in the marketplace because they were unemployed. Christianity sees life steadily and sees it whole, the seamy side as well as the "right" side.

But there is more to Christianity than realism. There is a Cross. In the events that lead to the crucifixion Jesus felt in his own body all the evils that flesh is heir to. But Jesus did not simply speculate about the problem of evil, or view it with the philosopher's cool detachment, nor did he merely endure it. He came to grips with the powers of evil in personal, hand-to-hand encounter and earned the right to say to his disciples, "In the world ye shall have tribulation, but be of good cheer, for I have overcome the world."

And so Paul, in our text today, sees the light of hope shining in the darkness of pain, suffering, tribulation, and persecution. "I consider that the sufferings of this present time are not worth comparing with the glory that is to be revealed to us." "This also shall pass away."

Our third point about hope can be illustrated by an experience of a friend of mine. He was sitting quietly in the seminary chapel one day before the service began. It was a gray day, and something of melancholy and sadness seemed to fill the air. Then, for just a moment, the sun broke through the clouds and for a fleeting moment touched the altar with glory. To my friend it was as though it were a sign.

Paul sees the sign of hope, that ray of light, touching with glory not only the sufferings of men and the darkness of a world, but the darkness of his own heart. "We know that the whole creation has been groaning in travail together until now; and not only the creation but we ourselves, who have the firstfruits of the Spirit, groan inwardly as we wait for adoption as sons, the redemption of our bodies. For in this hope we were saved." There was one thing that Paul was sure of—that he was saved. He was a Christian. God had called him on the Damascus Road. He had enlightened him with his gifts. But at the same time he was sure that he was not yet fully a Christian. He had a long way to go. Rather than being a discouragement, that was an encouraging thought. God who had begun a good work in him would go on finishing it until the day of Jesus Christ. It was only a beginning, but a beginning with a promise of the end. The best was yet to be. Paul looked back to D-Day—the day of resurrection—and he knew that He who had won that victory over the powers of sin and death would yet celebrate the final V-Day, when God would say, "It is finished."

Remember the old, old story of Pandora. It was she who opened, out of curiosity, Epimetheus' wallet, and let all man's blessings escape from it—all but one. When they looked, she found one blessing was left—it was hope.

> Why restless, why cast down, my soul?
> Hope still; and thou shalt sing
> The praise of him who is thy God
> Thy health's eternal Spring.

# SHOULDER YOUR PACK

## (*Labor Sunday*)

"Bear ye one another's burdens, and so fulfil the law of Christ"—Galatians 6:2.

DR. ALBERT SCHWEITZER, who is today's Number One world Christian, found when he first went to Africa as a doctor that there was neither office, dispensary, hospital, nor operating room that could be used. So before he could even begin to practice medicine he had to be in succession mason, carpenter and roofer with assorted building trades thrown in to boot. It was something of a sight to see a white man doing anything in that tropical hothouse but giving orders to natives, so he had no end of sidewalk superintendents standing about watching him working up a good sweat! After all he hadn't gone to Africa for his own health, so one day he accosted a splendid specimen of ebony manhood sitting in the shade of a nearby tree and asked him to lend a hand. The native shrugged a reply. "I'm an intellectual and don't drag wood about." "You're lucky" retorted the doctor. "I tried to be an intellectual, but didn't succeed."

The world in general has been divided between those people who *lift*, and those who *lean*. But there is no such division possible between Christians. There are no Christian leaners, only lifters. There is no such thing as an intellectual form of Christianity that doesn't soil its hands, or sweat its brow, or bend its back. There's no way to succeed in trying to become any other kind of Christian. Schweitzer knew what he was talking about. So does the Lord Jesus Christ. So does Paul.

For that's what Paul is talking about in our text for today when he calls to us: "Bear ye one another's burdens!" What kind of burdens do you mean, Paul?

"Brethren, if a man be overtaken in a fault . . ." Let's stop there to begin with. Just what does one do when a man or woman slips and falls? The story is told of a man who entered a minister's study one night, and asked whether he might talk with him alone. Obviously distraught and burdened in his mind, he needed help. Immediately, he came to the point and blurted out, "I have just killed a man." The minister asked his visitor to excuse him a moment then stepped into the other room where there was a telephone. He asked the operator to connect him with police headquarters. But when he came back the man was gone. A few minutes later the same man was in another minister's office down the street at a neighboring church. When he made his confession, "I have killed a man," the minister seemed not at all shocked, but settled back in his chair and asked, sympathetically, "Only once, my son, you have done this? Tell me about it."

The office of a Christian is not to be judge or jury, but to be a burden bearer. The prime duty of a Christian is to heal souls as a doctor's is to mend broken bones. "Brethren, if a man be overtaken in a fault, ye which are spiritual, restore such an one in the spirit of meekness."

Could the man who wrote those words be talking from past experience? Indeed so. How could Paul ever forget that hour in his own life when he himself had been overtaken by his sins on the Damascus Road—the white light of eter-

nity beating about him pitilessly, and the voice more terrible than the voice of conscience asking "Saul, Saul, why
persecutest thou me?" There he lay at Damascus, blind,
bewildered, miserably alone, when Ananias came to him
and, laying his hand upon him said "Brother Saul . . . the
Lord Jesus . . . hath sent me." As long as he lived the
great apostle would cherish those kind words, "Brother
Saul." They were balm to his spirit; they restored his soul;
his burden was shared by another.

Men are not always sinning, but there are other burdens
they lug through life. The burden of sorrow—what a griev-
ious load that is when it has to be carried alone. But sorrow
shared is sorrow divided. This is a truth that can be understood even by the very young. Children love the old story of
the king who one evening long ago—near Christmas time—
stood looking out his window at the deep, crisp snow.
Everyone was glad to be indoors and sit by the big fire piled
with logs in the hall. Presently the king called a little page
boy to his side. "Stand by me," said the king, "and tell me
who that man is picking up sticks?" The page looked out.
The moon was shining and the stars were out, and the snow
shown in the moonlight. "I know who he is," the page
said. "He lives a long way off, in a cottage on the other
side of the wood." Now the page's master had a loving
heart. It made him sad to think of anyone's being cold or
hungry. "Run and get some food . . . and some logs," he
said to the page, "then you and I will go and take them to
that poor man and his family." It was very cold and the
snow was deep, and it seemed such a long way to the poor
man's home on the other side of the wood. But when at
last they came to the cottage, how surprised the poor man

and his children were to see them, and how glad good king Wenceslas and his page were to help the poor and hungry.

You and I will have the opportunity in one way or another during the weeks ahead to do the very same thing for people who are cold and hungry. You and I will have the joy of sharing other people's burdens and so fulfilling the law of Christ. Perhaps this opportunity will come from a chance to donate old but still useful clothing or shoes for shipment to less fortunate people. Perhaps there will be an occasion to make a donation to some necessary relief project overseas. Perhaps this invitation to share will be an opportunity to inform ourselves on what needs there actually are in the world around us.

The absence of this spirit of responsibility and of sharing is what makes the headlines in our papers so black and the news that pours out of our radios so bleak. If Paul were revising the letter to the Galatians today I think he would add a P. S. to what he has already written. "Brethren, if a man be overtaken in a fault, ye that are spiritual, restore such an one in the spirit of meekness; considering thyself, lest thou also be tempted. Bear ye one another's burdens ... *Moreover, brethren, if a nation like Russia be overtaken in a fault, consider thyself, lest ye also be tempted.*"

The fearful cleavage in the public life of nations today, as always, springs from what someone has called "the moralism of the unconverted." The unconverted person dares not admit that he has faults, or has made mistakes in the past, or that he may possibly be in the wrong in the future. His time is too fully occupied denouncing the follies and stupidities of the party of the second part. It never occurs to him to consider the frailties of human nature with the aid of a mirror instead of a magnifying glass.

Nations get into the same predicament, hypocritically pointing out the faults and shortcomings of the countries for which they feel no love. Certainly no one in his right mind would want to claim that the communist leadership which controls Russia and China is democratic, benevolent and characterized by "sweetness and light." But we are not advancing the urgent necessity for world peace when we pretend that all virtue is to be found on our side of the Curtain, and all vice on the other. One of the greatest difficulties in creating an atmosphere where peace can be a reasonable expectation is the strange madness that seizes statesmen and beclouds the ordinary man's thinking when he assumes in the realm of politics and international relations that "I am pure and white but you are dirty and underhanded," in short, "the moralism of the unconverted."

A contrasting item from a Philadelphia newspaper reported that the American Friends Service Committee presented $25,000 worth of streptomycin to the people of Russia as a testimony of good will. It was to be handled by the Russian Red Cross, and was accompanied by this statement, "It is hoped that this may be the first of a series of reciprocal gestures between Russians and Americans which will lead them and us to more understanding." What if that type of a gesture would prove in the end to be more practical politics than the "get tough with Russia" school of politics? It would not be the first time that the realists proved to be the so-called impractical folk!

Again, what better Labor Sunday manifesto could there

be than these stirring words of Paul, "Bear ye one another's burdens"? Some people may feel that such a concern is none of the church's business. If they mean that the church ought not to take sides, they are, of course, right; but if they mean that the church should be aloof from this burning issue, they are dead wrong. Nothing human can really be alien to the church of Jesus Christ.

A recurring pattern in the affairs of industry reminds one somewhat of the cartoon showing two English fishwives standing on the front stoops of their respective houses and hurling insults at each other across the street. The shrewd comment beneath the picture was, "They'll never get together. They're arguing from different premises." But what if this is all a tragic illusion? What if labor and management were really living in the same house. What if they should start with this premise: We are members one of another. Actually there is no difference between the apparently contradictory slogans "The most wages for the least work" and "The most work for the least wages." If the former is in the ascendant now, it's only the other end of the pendulum swing. As in the political world, so too in the economic world—relations have been poisoned by the "*im*moralism of the unconverted" which puts the burden of responsibility on the other fellow for the ills of social life.

It is a hopeful sign when representative leaders of management and labor like Paul G. Hoffman and Walter P. Reuther can join in issuing a Labor Sunday message as they did one year recently. Here are a few significant sentences: "The church is under a divine imperative to call all men—but first its own members—to recognize God's lordship over individual souls and the whole of life. . . . It is His will that His Kingdom come on earth among men. . . . Every form of human ownership or control or use of property is a trust with responsibility to God and one's fellow men. . . . Hence, the worker must never be treated as a commodity but always as a person. . . . No economic system fully serves the common good. No such system fully expresses the will of God. Improvement of economic arrangement is, therefore, the obligation of all Christians. . . . Christians who share in the control of economic power, whether in management or as representatives of organized labor, have a special responsibility to direct economic forces toward service to the whole society. . . . Labor Sunday presents a clear call to every Christian to consider earnestly the possibility and the means of attaining a more Christian economic life than now exists."

So no area of life—from the life of the individual in his sin, his sorrow, his suffering, on to the complexities of social life, international relations, labor relations—can be exempt from this law of Christ which we are called to fulfill: Bear ye one another's burdens.

But did you notice how, only two sentences later on in Galatians, Paul apparently takes back what he has just said. "For every man shall bear his own burden." Now what can he mean contradicting himself like that? Might it be not contradiction, but a deeper insight? Everything that is accomplished for good and God comes because someone says, face to face with some great task, "Here am I, Lord, send me."

Light looked down and beheld darkness:
"Thither will I go," said Light.
Peace looked down and beheld War:
"Thither will I go," said Peace.
Love looked down and beheld hatred:
"Thither will I go," said Love.[6]

Paul didn't say, "Pack up your troubles in your old kit bag and smile, smile, smile" but something like this: "Shoulder your kit and march, march, march!"

That word *burden* is the same word that sailors use for cargo, and soldiers use for their equipment. Every man has his own pack to carry. Certain things are going to be done only when you shoulder your pack and start marching. How much Kingdom cargo can you carry?

The success of every church, humanly speaking, depends on just one thing—the size of the number of those who are willing to carry the burden of responsibility by active participation. There is work here that will not be done unless you shoulder your pack. This is a pastor's constant prayer, that you will be willing—a great congregation, marching shoulder to shoulder bearing one another's burdens. Let us not ask "for tasks equal to our strength, but for strength equal to our tasks."

# REDEEMED BY FIRE

## (*Pentecost*)

ONE OF the great narratives in the Old Testament is the story of the intercession of Abraham for the city of Sodom. Having heard that the wickedness of the city was very great, the Lord sent two angelic messengers to see whether the report was true. "Then Abraham drew near, and said, 'Wilt thou indeed destroy the righteous with the wicked? Suppose there are fifty righteous within the city; wilt thou then destroy the place and not spare it for the fifty righteous who are in it? . . . Shall not the Judge of all the earth do right?' And the Lord said, 'If I find at Sodom fifty righteous in the city, I will spare the whole place for their sake.'

"Abraham answered, 'Behold, I have taken upon myself to speak to the Lord, I who am but dust and ashes. Suppose five of the fifty righteous are lacking? Wilt thou destroy the whole city for lack of five?' And he said, 'I will not destroy it if I find forty-five there.' Again he spoke to him, and said, 'Suppose forty are found there.' He answered, 'For the sake of forty I will not do it.' Then he said, 'Oh let not the Lord be angry, and I will speak. Suppose thirty are found there.' He answered, 'I will not do it if I find thirty there.'" And as Abraham continued to intercede the figure shrank to twenty. Finally Abraham said, "'Oh let not the Lord be angry, and I will speak again but this once. Suppose ten are found there.' He answered, 'For the sake of ten I will not destroy it.'" (Cf. Gen. 18:22-33, R.S.V.)

But you know what happened. There were *not* ten righteous people there. No not one. So fire fell from heaven, and Sodom and Gomorrah became a place of desolation on the map, and a paragraph in the history of man.

But this ancient story has a way of coming alive. There are those among us who seem to be saying that Sodom is a symbol. It stands for a city, any city or civilization over which hangs the threat of destruction. Our own government is preoccupied with the problem—the realization that what happened to Sodom long ago, and what happened to Hiroshima and Nagasaki, can happen to us. It can happen here. One writer in a news magazine described the tense world situation as being like two gamblers quarreling over a card table, each man sitting three feet from his opponent with gun drawn and finger on trigger. But neither dares to pull the trigger, knowing full well that if he fires first, the fatal shot will produce a muscular reaction that will discharge the other pistol, and would thus mean the end for himself as well.

It was this human situation that T. S. Eliot had in mind when he wrote those cryptic lines:

> The only hope, or else despair
>   Lies in the choice of pyre or pyre—
> To be redeemed from fire by fire . . .
>   We only live, only suspire
> Consumed by either fire or fire.[7]

What does he mean by that? The story of the first Pentecost describes how holy fire fell from heaven upon the heads of the disciples who were waiting for the promise of the Holy Spirit. When this redeeming fire had fallen, then the prayer of Abraham was answered. Ten righteous men, plus one other, were indeed found who were empowered to save the world from destruction by the fire of God's wrath. The hope of our world is the church of the living God, but a church which is itself on fire. Can Pentecost be repeated? Can Pentecostal flames descend once more upon *our* heads?

If the old story of Pentecost is not simply ancient history, how does it apply to us today? Redeeming fire fell *first* upon a *waiting* church. The disciples had been instructed to tarry in Jerusalem until they had received the promise of the Father. But while they waited, they were not just passing the time. They waited, and also waited on God in prayer. "As they mused, the fire burned." They were with one accord in the temple worshiping. They were searching the scriptures to see how they could square their faith in the Crucified Lord with the ancient scripture of the Jewish people. It was not a passive waiting, but a highly active waiting. Then when the day of Pentecost fully came— redeeming fire fell upon the waiting church.

Second, the flames of Pentecost fell upon a *united* church. Again and again the record stresses the fact of their unity. They were of one heart and one mind. They felt so much at one that they even for a time broke down the barriers between "mine and thine." They had all things in common. The sense of unity broke down the ancient differences between race and race. Fifteen nations are mentioned: the men of the ancient East, Parthians, Medes, Elamites, and dwellers in Mesopotamia, Hellas, Italy, and Africa. They all heard in their own tongue the wonderful works of God. Here was the first League of Nations. Here the United

Nations became a fact. In Christ there is no East or West, no South or North, but one great brotherhood of men, around the whole wide earth. It was a united church, as well as a waiting church, upon which redeeming fire fell. How long will we grieve the Spirit of God by persisting in our sorry divisions?

Third, fire fell upon a *witnessing* church. The church of Pentecost was a church on fire. It knew why it was there—to be the light of the world, a lamp set on a stand, not under a bushel. A church that has lost its power of witnessing is as useless as a red warning flag that has been bleached white by the sun. Bishop Gerald Kennedy, from his nationwide experience in dealing with many churches and church people within and without his own communion, gives it as his judgment that too large a proportion of people, except in the despised and lowly fringe movements, have lost their faith in the power of the gospel to transform and redeem life. Yet as you read the sermon in Acts you can put the aim of every sermon into one sentence: The aim of this sermon is to get a decision for Jesus Christ, the hope of the world. The church was on fire with redeeming fire.

Fourth, this sense of witnessing—which was manifested in Peter's great sermon on Pentecost, in Paul's sermon on Mars Hill, and in Stephen's valiant testimony before the Sanhedrin—was not confined to the leaders alone. Everybody had a sense of individual responsibility to speak the Word of Jesus Christ. The fire of the Holy Spirit fell not just on Peter, James, and John, but upon them all. Peter could think only of the wonderful prophecy which came to fulfilment thus: ". . . your young men shall see visions, and your old men shall dream dreams. . . . I will pour out my Spirit upon all flesh."

We must recover this sense of individual responsibility today. Opportunities for personal witness arise constantly if we can only have the wit to take the cue. A well-known clergyman was a guest recently on a very popular nationally broadcast TV program in which he was given an eight-minute "slot" of time to answer certain questions of general interest in the field of religion. Arriving at the studio he was given a few minutes to glance at the questions. But when the MC reached the end of the questions at the end of the precious eight minutes (at how many thousands of dollars a minute!) the questions kept coming, questions that weren't on the typed list at all. They were the MC's own probing, personal questions. Before millions of people unaware of what was going on, the old, old, question was being asked, and answered: "What must I do to be saved?" It was another case of "one believing heart setting another on fire."

Fifth—the fire that fell from heaven upon the waiting disciples was the fire of fervor and enthusiasm. Again and again we find its manifestations in the single-heartedness of a Paul saying, "This one thing I do, forgetting the things that are behind, I press on to the mark for the prize of the high calling of God in Christ Jesus." Bruce Barton said once, "If you can give your son only one gift, let it be enthusiasm." Well, those first Christians were enthusiastic. A distinguished university professor said that one of the sad things about educating people by the hundreds of thousands is that we educate the enthusiasm out of them. Education tends to make a man cautious, aloof, inclined to weigh the arguments on both sides of any issue—and not to commit himself, if he can help it.

But whenever Pentecost has come to the Christian church, Christianity has been a power which has stirred the imagination, and kindled the fires of passion, of devotion, and enthusiasm. "Savonarola has a passion (an enthusiasm) in his soul for Christ, and Florence shouts for an hour, 'We will have no king but Christ!' John Wesley has a passion in his soul for Christ, and all England comes to a new sense of God. William Booth has a passion in his soul for Christ, and the Salvation Army is still saying to every person it reaches, however poor and defeated, 'God is!' "[8]

The sixth mark of the Pentecostal fire was that it was redeeming fire, the fire of God's compassion and love. God does not will the death of the sinner, but that the sinner should turn from the error of his way and live. God does not delight in the destruction of Sodom and Gomorrah, any more than he would be pleased with the destruction of any of the great cities on this side or the other side of the Iron Curtain. His wrath is only the other side of his love. But his love is also the other side of his wrath, his steady resistance to evil, iniquity, and sin.

A few days ago I was reminded of the old story of Absalom, the son of David who revolted against his father, the king, and who made his father flee from Jerusalem and the throne. Son finally met father on the field of battle— the young ambitious and rebellious son and the wily old veteran of many a conflict and campaign. Reluctant as he was to fight, David could not allow rebellion, but he still gave orders to deal gently with the erring prodigal. You remember what happened. Absalom was defeated in battle

and fled, but in his flight he was caught in the branches of
a tree and was slain by Joab. Meanwhile, David sat in the
gate awaiting tidings of the battle. A man came running.
The watchman called out and told the king. The king said
"If he is alone, there are tidings in his mouth." He drew
near, and behind him another man came running. The first
man burst upon the scene and cried, "All is well," but when
the king asked about Absalom he lied and said he did not
know. Meanwhile, the second man came with his tidings,
and when the king asked, "Is it well with the young man
Absalom," he blurted out the truth. The king was deeply
moved and went to his room over the gate and wept. As he
went he said, "O my son Absalom, my son, my son Absalom! Would I had died instead of you, O Absalom, my son,
my son!"

The tidings we have to bring to the world are not bad
news, but good news. News of a king's son who died for
love of us all, whose love has a wideness like the wideness
of the sea, redeeming the world by fire from fire.

> Come, Holy Ghost, our souls inspire
> And lighten with celestial fire;
> Thou the anointing Spirit art
> Who dost thy sevenfold gifts impart.
>
> Thy blessed unction from above
> Is comfort, life, and fire of love.
> Enable with perpetual light
> The dullness of our blinded sight.

# THE BRIGHT GLORY OF CHRISTMAS

"God, who at sundry times and in divers manners spake in time past unto the fathers by the prophets, hath in these last days spoken unto us by his Son, whom he hath appointed heir of all things, by whom also he made the worlds; who being the brightness of his glory, and the express image of his person, and upholding all things by the word of his power, when he had by himself purged our sins, sat down on the right hand of the Majesty on high"—Hebrews 1:1-3.

WAITING FOR Christmas to come when you are very young is like waiting for a delayed train in a railroad station. You keep looking and looking down the track, and it just *never* seems to come. But as you grow older the passing years seem to speed by like telegraph poles when you are riding in the train, slipping away into the past until they merge at the vanishing point of the horizon.

I am sure that each of us has memories of past Christmases that stand out and have a kind of timeless quality that makes their remembrance as fresh today as the day we experienced them. One that stands out in personal recollection was the Christmas I spent abroad as an exchange student. With genuine Christian hospitality a German family opened wide their doors to make a happy Christmas for three Americans whose holiday would otherwise have been drab and lonely and miserable indeed. It was a veritable story-book Christmas from the moment we stepped into the noble Gothic church which had looked down upon nearly seven hundred Christmas celebrations—a church which had heard the voice of Martin Luther and had watched Napoleon three hundred years later when that little man had his brief hour upon the stage of history. Wending our way home, snow was falling in great flakes, while from the church belfry carols fell like a benediction upon the quiet village. Then there was the Christmas dinner in the dining-room, cozy in the warmth of the great porcelain stove, and the moment for which the grandchildren had been waiting—the coming of *Christkind* who vanished as mysteriously as he had come. But with it all something was missing. Then it came, what I had been waiting for. There was a knock at the door and the familiar yellow envelope—a cablegram with a brief message from loved ones at home. Only then was Christmas really complete.

To spend Christmas in a far away place without a word from home, with not so much as a greeting card from father or mother, that is the quintessence of misery. Is it not precisely this that makes Christmas so glorious for us who dwell on earth that there comes to us good tidings from the Eternal Father's house, the gospel of the love of God in Jesus Christ? Christians are so rich in having God's Word that they can scarcely imagine how impoverished they would be without it. It might help us to realize our blessings if we could only imagine what it would be like had the heavens never been rent asunder, had no babe ever been found by those who sought him. What would it be like to have no sense of direction of whence we come and whither we go? As we contemplate such misery we begin to grasp what a glorious gospel is proclaimed to us in our scripture text for today: "God hath spoken to us in his Son."

Our Christmas text is written in the opening words of the Epistle to the Hebrews in words that have something of the grandeur and rhythm of a noble hymn played upon a mighty organ. The author takes us by the hand and bids us watch a long procession moving through the ages, the patriarch Abraham, standing under a star-studded sky, motionless, waiting in an attitude of prayer, who heard a voice that said to him, "Go from your country and your kindred and your father's house to the land that I will show you." (R.S.V.) So Abraham went as the Lord had told him. Then Moses also heard a voice that bade him go and overrode every objection, "Go, tell Pharaoh to let my people go." And after the patriarchs the long procession of the prophets, Amos and Micah, Hosea, and Isaiah, Jeremiah and Ezekiel, and each of them with a different message, but with each of them the burden was the same, "Thus saith the Lord." God hath spoken. In many and various ways God spoke of old to our fathers by the prophets.

Now this procession wends its way to a little village. The prophet had spoken of it, "But you, O Bethlehem . . . who are little to be among the clans of Judah, from you shall come forth for me one who is to be ruler in Israel, whose origin is from of old, from ancient days." (R.S.V.) Like the prophets, this one had a word from the Lord, but there was a difference. He spoke with authority. "It hath been said to you by them of old . . . but I say." The prophets had a word from the Lord. He was himself the Word. "In many and various ways God spoke of old to our fathers by the prophets; but in these last days he has spoken to us by a Son, whom he appointed the heir of all things. . . . He reflects the glory of God and bears the very stamp of his nature, upholding the universe by his word of power. When he had made purification for sins, he sat down at the right hand of the Majesty on high. . . ." (R.S.V.)

What does it mean to say that God has spoken to us? It means that God does not remain aloof and remote, throned upon the clouds indifferent to what takes place on earth, and content to leave the world to go its merry way to hell and destruction. You remember Carlyle's famous description of the philosopher sitting in his cell high and lifted up above the noise and clamor, the getting and the spending, the living and the dying of the ordinary mortals who lived in the myriad dwellings in the city spread out at his feet. It was beneath him, in more than one sense. He dwelt apart with his books and his ideas. He felt more at home with the fathers in their dusty tomes, than with the children of men down yonder. But God is not aloof. He cares. He cannot keep silence and let men go unwarned into the ways of sin and death.

When we say God has spoken to us, it means that God acts in his Word. His Word is a call to decision. God does not speak in the indicative mood so much as in the imperative: "Follow me." His Word is creative—and causative. "Let there be light!"

When we say, "God speaks," it means that he comes into personal relations with us. He gives himself to us in fellowship. He treats us not as pawns upon life's checkerboard, but as persons who can respond and understand.

All this is what is meant by Christmas. The Word was made flesh and dwelt among us, and we beheld his glory—glory as of the only-begotten of the Father, full of grace and truth. For this cause we preach, for this reason we sing our carols, because of this we can pray, Our Father, because God has spoken to us in the one whose birth we celebrate at Christmas.

In his eagerness to express the full scope and wonder of the Christmas gift, our author tells us that Jesus reflects the glory of God. We cannot bear to look directly into the noonday sun in its glory, but when we see the setting sun, veiled by clouds, and glimpse the radiance as it shines, or see the moon in the night sky and know that its radiance is borrowed light, we begin to understand what our author means. "No man hath seen God at any time; the only begotten Son . . . he hath declared him." "He that hath seen me hath seen the Father," is our Lord's own word.

But even that cannot fully satisfy the sacred writer, so he tries again: "He bears the very stamp of (God's) nature." Just as the wax bears the faithful impression of the king's ring, so Christ manifests the character of God.

Now the procession moves on. This procession, that had begun with Abraham and the prophets and continued until it reached Bethlehem, moves on until it reaches a place called Calvary. The blinding brightness of Christmas is this fact that passes understanding: Immanuel, God with us, is also our Saviour, God for us, who for us men and our salvation came down from heaven, and was incarnate by the Virgin Mary and was made man, and was crucified also for us under Pontius Pilate. The end of the road is not Bethlehem, but Calvary.

You remember that beautiful legend of the shepherd who having no worthy gift like the Wise Men from the east, made a little cross of broken twigs, as a little toy. And Mary, speaking to the babe, bade him choose the one that pleased him the best. And the babe with divine wisdom was not tempted by the glitter of the gold nor any other gifts of the Wise Men, but chose instead the shepherd's poor gift of crossed twigs.[9] This is legend, to be sure, but legends often embody divine truth. The Incarnation is fully understood only when we come to Calvary.

"When he had made purification for sins, he sat down at the right hand of Majesty on high." There the road ends—in the Father's house.

> For men are homesick in their homes
> And strangers under the sun,
> And they lay their heads in a foreign land
> When ever the day is done. . . .
>
> There fared a mother driven forth
> Out of an inn to roam;
> In the place where she was homeless
> All men are at home.
> The crazy stable close at hand,
> With shaking timber and shifting sand,
> Grew a stronger thing to abide and stand
> Than the square stones of Rome.

And so . . .

> To an open house in the evening
> Home shall men come,
> To an older place than Eden
> And a taller town that Rome.
> To the end of the way of the wandering star,
> To the place the things that cannot be and that are,
> To the place where God was homeless
> And all men are at home.[10]

# THE FINE ART OF BLOTTING

BEN JOHNSON said once that Shakespeare would have been even greater than he was, *"If* he had not forgot that last and greatest art—the art *to blot."*

What did he mean by that? The blotter—that thing you look for so often while the ink is drying—is a rather recent invention. It used to be that when you blotted something, you obliterated it, struck it out with your pen, made marks through it so no one could read what was there before. The grocer, for example, used to keep his accounts in a big ledger. When you paid your bill, he just crossed it out with great sweeping x's. That was blotting. That is what the Bible tells us God has done with our accounts, which were overdue and unpaid until Someone paid them for us and crossed out what was charged against us.

The world would be a far better place, and a happier place to live in, if we who are followers of Christ would just practice that "fine art to blot." I would like to suggest that this is what the Apostle Paul had in mind when he bade us forget the things which are behind. In these uncertain days a good many people are worried about the future, and not without cause, surely. But I'd like to suggest that for no small number of people the past is almost as great a problem as the future. Somewhere along the way Paul faced this problem squarely. The fine art of blotting is an important part of any design for living. I can hear Paul say "There are some rules you must observe in practicing the art of blotting, and rule

74

number one is: 'Forget how good you once thought you were.'"

Once upon a time Paul had entertained a pretty good opinion of himself. As you know, he was born a Jew, and he was proud of it. He traced his ancestry back to the tribe of Benjamin—which hadn't much to boast of when it came to numbers, but did have kings in the family tree. So, royal blood flowed in his veins. He was a Hebrew of the Hebrews, a Pharisee of the Pharisees. On that exclusive avenue of moral perfectionism, he lived in the last house!

But, why does Paul *now* want to forget all this proud past? Why does he want to "blot it out"? Because, in an hour of soul refining, beaten down to earth by the white light of eternity on the Damascus road, he came to realize that the goodness of which he had been so proud was not a religious asset but actually a liability. As long as a man is under the mistaken impression that flushed cheeks and a high temperature are a sign of health, you can't get him to go to bed or send for a doctor. As Jesus put it, "Those who are well have no need of a physician, but those who are sick." Paul *now* looked upon his past, with all its feverish activity, as a sickness from which he had been delivered by the help of the Great Physician.

Experience bears out his discovery. It is to those who sense their own poverty of spirit that Christ comes in all his richness. It is to those who know that they are empty vessels, that Christ comes to fill that void. It is when a drowning man gives up the struggle that the Life Guard can come near and save him. Thus it is only when a man gives up remembering how good he thinks he is, that the good Lord has a chance to make a better man of him. If the past is to live anywhere, it should live in our conscience, rather than in our imagination.

Who were the people who gave our Lord the most trouble? Not the thugs and the bad actors, but those who were "good" and couldn't forget it.

You remember that rich young ruler who came to Jesus asking what he should do to inherit eternal life. When Jesus checked up on how he'd kept the Ten Commandments, the youth kept saying "I've done that. I've kept that. This is nothing new to me, I've observed all that from my youth up." But when Jesus suggested that he go on from there and do a heroic deed that would take hold of his selfishness at the very root, he went away sorrowful. Why? Because his goodness was all in the *past*. He wasn't looking for any more worlds to conquer. He had arrived, but refused to "blot out" the achievements of the past.

I wonder if there isn't a little of that Jack Horner spirit in all of us, willingness to reach into the past and pull out the plums of achievement and say, "What a good boy am I." Of Pitt, the English statesman, someone made the scathing observation, "He did not grow, he was cast." At forty he was the same man he had been at twenty. He had not increased in wisdom, or moral stature, or in favor with God or man. Yet as Augustine observed long ago, "Not to advance is to retreat." If you and I are serious about the better life, we must practice that last and greatest art— the art of blotting out the memory of past achievement.

Now let us add to rule number one: "Forget how good you thought you were," a second rule, the very opposite of the first. The fine art of blotting consists also in forgetting how *bad* you know you were. This is fully as important as the other.

An enterprising agent approached Themistocles, the Athenian statesman, and offered him a system of memory training so perfect that he promised him he would be able to remember *any*thing he wished to remember. But the badgered statesman refused the offer, saying, "Oh, how happy I should be if you could teach me to *forget* the things I want to forget." So that was a problem in 500 B.C. too!

If thousands of lives are spoiled by too fond and too frequent recollection of how good they once thought they were, tens of thousands of lives are literally wrecked by inability to forget how bad they know they were. Those twin demons—worry and the sense of unrelieved guilt—can become so deep-seated that they can be removed only by drastic shock treatment in a mental hospital. When the roots of the trouble are exposed and removed, then health of body and mind can be restored again.

But if the truth were known, *most* people live lives of quiet desperation. How many of us right now are saying something like this to ourselves: "If *I* could only forget the things I would like to forget. Memories that pursue me into my dreams, failures and treacheries, weak compromises, places I avoid because of the memories they stir; people I avoid for the same reason; things not done that I should have done. I am haunted, night and day, by all the things I have not done. Oh, to be able to blot them all out."

Is there any way to deal effectively with that marred past? The only way we can deal with it is by resolving to do better the next time. We can be scrupulously honest in the future, if we have been careless with the truth before.

Indeed, our only chance against failure and sin really is in being shocked by it. But the record of the past stands, and by the very laws of being, what I have written affects the *present* too. We know that the future cannot alter the past. What then?

The Bible tells us God has done something about the past, and he will do something about it for us, *if we will only let him.* In the Old Testament God promised, "I will forgive their iniquities, and remember their sin no more." The prophet Jeremiah held out the wonderful prospect that the days would come when men would look for that soiled and spotted record and would not be able to find it, because God had completely "blotted it out" of the book of his remembrance. That ancient promise is kept at the Cross. The good news of the gospel is the assurance that God has "blotted out" the handwriting that was against us.

So a man like Paul, haunted for years by a bad conscience, and the bitter memories of failure, the savage persecution of helpless people, and even hands dyed with the blood of legal murder, can now go blithely on his way, "Forgetting what lies behind." What God did for me, says Paul, he is surely able to do for you too, weaving it into his pattern, his design for living.

After that, we can add this third rule. In the fine art of blotting, you must learn to forget the little rankling wrongs that others have done to you.

When you were a child I wonder if you sometimes made little baskets out of thistle pods? Those great burrs had needle-sharp points. You could stick them together and easily make a basket. Well, a good many people go through life like those baskets, all prickly without, and full to the brim with resentments. They are the people who tell you they are always getting the raw deals, who never get any breaks, whose shoulders are always carrying a chip of some kind. Unless I'm mistaken, we've got to be careful in these tense days lest we be turned into a nation of grumblers and faultfinders and grudge-bearers. What we need is poorer memories. What we need is someone who can teach us how to forget. What some of us need is a brand-new blotter. God has an unlimited supply of them *if* we will only seek and ask.

There was once a general named Marcus Aurelius. He was really an emperor, but he spent more time in his campaign tent than he ever did in his palace. I have no doubt he was tempted often enough to indulge in what has ever been the soldier's prerogative—to gripe about things. But listen to what he says in his *Meditations*. "*Forget* the offence and you will forget the offender. Forget the *offender* and the offence ceases to be." That's blotting of the right sort, forgetting the things which are behind and letting them stay there in the past where they belong. Yes . . .

> Let us forget the things that vexed and tried us,
> The worrying things that caused our souls to fret;
> The hopes that, cherished long, were *still* denied us
>     Let us forget.
> Let us forget the little slights that pained us,
> The *greater* wrongs that rankle sometimes yet;
> The pride with which some lofty one disdained us
>     Let us forget.

Let no one think, however, that what we are advocating is complete irresponsibility towards man's inhumanity to man. I dare *not* blot out the memory of the wrongs and injustices my neighbor suffers. So Paul, who says that as for himself he can forgive and forget, cries out, "Who is weak, and I am not weak? Who is offended and I burn not?" We are here to see that the weak and helpless are not imposed upon.

We have come so far then. You agree, it's a good thing to forget how good you used to think you were; and a better thing to forget how bad you know you were; and very commendable indeed to forget the petty annoyances, which like sand in a shoe can become irritating and make you irritable. But how are you going to do all these things? Someone has said that "how" is apt to be the forgotten word in the preacher's vocabulary—and not only the preacher's vocabulary. Here, too, Paul is ready with his answer. Forgetting what lies behind comes from a change of direction, an about-face—"Straining forward to what lies ahead, I press on toward the goal for the prize of the upward call of God in Christ Jesus." (R.S.V.) Paul had learned that life's *ultimate wisdom is in choosing what you wish to remember*. Many unpleasant things had come his way in life: prison, humiliation, mistreatment, and injustice. But all that is forgotten now. Listen to him here as he tells the Philippians the things he prefers to remember: "Whatsoever things are true . . . honest . . . just . . . pure . . . lovely . . . of good report; if there be any virtue, and if there be any praise, think on these things." (A.V.)

Best of all there was Christ, true, honest, just, and fairest of ten thousand. Not an ideal only, but an ideal incarnate, a person and a presence. Robert Browning had been telling some people how he first met Shelley, the poet who inspired him, gave him friendship, and fanned the spark of genius into flame. That day stood out from all others. But they, not realizing what that friendship meant, said, "How interesting. Tell us what else happened that day when you walked on the moors together?" "What else?" asked Browning, doubting his ears, "What else?"

I crossed a moor, with a name of its own
    And a certain use in the world no doubt,
Yet a hand's-breadth of it shines alone
    'Mid the blank miles round about;

For there I picked up on the heather,
    And there I put inside my breast
A molted feather, an eagle-feather!
    Well, I forget the rest.

So say they too, who have Christ as friend and Master— "Well, I forget the rest."

# BRIGHT SHOOTS OF EVERLASTINGNESS

## (*Transfiguration*)

"And I turned to see the voice that spake with me. And being turned, I saw seven golden candlesticks; and in the midst of the seven candlesticks one like unto the Son of man"
—Revelation 1:12–13.

DESPITE ITS gruesome title, Arthur Miller's play, *Death of a Salesman*, has made a profound impression upon many people. It tells the story of a traveling salesman who is always on the verge of, but never *quite* achieves success. Once he begins to slip, he has nothing to hold to or to hold him, and he can't admit to himself that he is a failure. So after several unsuccessful efforts he finally succeeds in committing suicide. Nobody comes to the funeral except his wife and two sons and one neighbor, Charley. As they turn to leave, the son who had never gotten along with his father says, "He had the wrong dreams, all, all wrong. He never knew who he was." But Charley defends him stoutly saying, "Nobody dast blame this man. Willy was a salesman. He's a man way out there in the blue, riding on a smile and a shoeshine. And when they start *not* smiling back— that's an earthquake. And then you get yourself a couple of spots on your hat, and you're finished. Nobody dast *blame* this man. . . ."[11]

What is the underlying message the playwright is trying to get across to us? Is he saying, as wise men have, that "nothing fails like success"? Does he mean that so-called success alone can never really satisfy—chrome, gadgets, the latest models, and all the outward and visible tokens of achievement? Is that what he means when he has the neighbor answer Willy's widow as he does? She can't *understand*, and says that they had almost gotten everything paid for, and that Willy only needed a *little* salary. So the neighbor says, "No man *only* needs a little salary"—or a lot of salary, for man shall not live by salary alone. It seems to me that the play is a vivid parable of the *peril* of emptiness. Willy had dreams—but not vision. He had a lusty body—but no soul. He had a code of honor but no ethics. He scolded his boy for stealing a football from the coach, but he was really proud of what he called the boy's initiative. In his book it was not wrong to do wrong—only to get caught. It would not be right to say Willy had no religion—though he used the Lord's name only for purposes of profanity. He had a god whose name was success, and when this god failed, he couldn't face the barren empty shell of life that was left. One has the uncomfortable feeling that Arthur Miller is holding a mirror up to life in twentieth-century America, and is asking us if we like what we see reflected there.

Long ago the prophet said, "Where there is no vision, the people perish." Today is Transfiguration Sunday, and both our Gospel (Matt. 17:1–9) and our text from the book of Revelation present to us visions that were granted to Peter, James, and John on the mountain top to which Jesus had taken them, and to John on his lonely Isle of Patmos. Here were men that were facing an earthquake too. Life was shortly to tumble in upon them. But it did not overwhelm them, because they carried in their hearts a vision of Christ. Soon their faith would suffer total eclipse—Jesus would be crucified, dead, and buried—but beyond the eclipse there was a vision splendid of a Christ not dead but alive, not defeated but triumphant, not impaled upon a cross, but seated upon a throne. Jesus is not simply the carpenter of Nazareth, not simply the teacher who spake as never man spake. He was and is God's Son, Light of light, very God of very God. Peter, James, and John now knew that they could never think too magnificently of Jesus—

> But felt through all this fleshly dress
> Bright shoots of everlastingness.[12]

It was this same vision splendid that came to John, indeed, it was the inspiration for his writing the book of Revelation. Because he was a Christian leader, and because the Christian religion of his day was *religio illicita* in the unholy Roman Empire, John had been banished from Ephesus to the barren, rock-bound Isle of Patmos in the Aegean Sea. But this forced separation became, under the Spirit of God, a service to his brethren on the mainland and a channel of blessing for the church of every land and every century since. "Why was I not exiled before?" asked Victor Hugo when he found that his enforced separation stirred the creative spirit to function within him. There he wrote those books which have secured him a place in literature that might possibly never have been his had this blessing in disguise never befallen him.

So John tells us that in his lonely island prison he was in the Spirit on the Lord's day, when he received the commission to write the book of Revelation and send it to the seven churches in Asia Minor.

Turning to see the one who was speaking to him he saw seven golden lampstands, and in the midst of the lampstands one like a son of man. What a wonderful vision—a Christ who is in the midst of his church, one like a son of man. Only this long-expected figure for which Israel had been praying since before the days of Daniel, this Messiah of the future is *the* Son of man, whose name is Jesus Christ, not one *still* to come, but one who *has* come, one who *is*, the Alpha and the Omega, the beginning and the end, one who died and, behold, is alive forever more, who holds in his nail-pierced hands the keys of death and Hades.

Three things in particular are the marks or attributes of the Son of man in John's vision.

First, he is clothed with a long robe and with a golden girdle round his breast. This description would be familiar to everyone conversant with Jewish worship. What John is describing is the high priest who once each year went within the holy of holies to make atonement for the sins of the people. But this is the difference: Christ is the High Priest in the *heavenly* places who made *one* sacrifice for the salvation of the world, who ever liveth to make inter-cession for his people before God. His whole countenance from head to foot is suffused with the white radiance of eternity, for God is light and in him is no darkness at all.

Second, in his vision John sees Christ as Prophet as well as Priest. The voice like the sound of many waters, and the sharp two-edged sword which issued forth from his mouth symbolize the one who utters the sure judgments of God, whose terrible swift sword executes judgment for all the oppressed. In the parable of the last judgment the Son of man speaks the word and humanity is divided into the two groups, infallibly and finally—and there is no appeal from his judgment: "Inasmuch as ye did it unto one of the least of these my brethren . . . Inasmuch as ye did it not . . ."

Third, in his vision John sees one who holds in his right hand the seven stars. This is the Beautiful Saviour, King and Lord of creation. In John's day astrology was one of the sciences, and men read the rise and fall of nations in the stars, and believed that a great man would have his great star, such as the Wise Men followed from the East. The Seven Stars, or the constellation of the Little Dipper, as we call it, were identified with the mighty world power of Rome and her empire. And here, said John, he saw one who held in his right hand the seven stars of Rome, all the might and glory of Rome herself. No wonder he cried out in that magnificent hymn in Revelation, "Worthy is the Lamb!"

Is it any wonder that John fell at the feet of Christ as though dead? Christ, Prophet, Priest, and King!

But someone may be saying to himself, "Visions—aren't they unreal, untrustworthy, visionary, mere constructs of pious fantasy and imagining? I've never seen a vision." To which the short and perfect squelch might be, "Don't you wish you could?"

Granted there are hallucinations, and pious imaginings, and that we should "prove the Spirit." Even the Church of Rome is wary and skeptical, and undertakes to question purported visions. It denied one in Wisconsin not long since, and has remained noncommittal about another purported vision in Fairmount Park, Philadelphia, as reported by several children.

Granted then that there may be pious frauds, and hallucinations, can anything positive be said about visions?

For one thing, the poets—those who are at home in the realm of the good, the true, and the beautiful—declare that there is a spiritual world as well as a material world. For

Peter Bell, "a yellow primrose by a river's brim was a yellow primrose and nothing more." But for the poet it was the outward and visible expression of a Spirit who created beauty. "Earth's crammed with heaven," cries Browning, "but only those who see take off their shoes, the rest sit around and eat blackberries."

But beyond that—there is evidence in history too—certainly something can be said for visions. One thinks of Joan of Arc, recanting when she was given the choice by the Inquisitor of denying that she had seen visions and heard voices. But from her prison cell later recanting her recantation, and bravely going to the stake, she said, "It is I who have failed, not my voices."

Moreover the Bible too is on the side of the angels. The hard-headed realist who is rooted to the world of sense must find certain sections of the Bible nonsense, and many parts of it a closed book, if he dismisses spiritual insight and vision as impossible. What then are we to make of Jesus' words, when the returning disciples reported their success, and he said, "I beheld Satan as lightning fall from heaven." What are we to make of Paul's vision of the Risen Christ on the Damascus road, something so overwhelming that it knocked him off his high-horse, and changed him from a persecutor to a prosecutor, from a foe to a friend of Christ? Spiritual things are spiritually discerned. The spiritually perceptive are able to see behind this earthly dress the bright shoots of everlastingness which those of us who are duller of comprehension cannot behold. Just as the Alpine mountaineer who was our guide to the glacier opposite the Matterhorn could see with his naked eye a party of mountain climbers as they neared the summit of the mountain peak, while I, even with field glasses had to look and look and look before I finally got the climbers in my field of vision.

The vision on the Mount of Transfiguration was not for everybody—but only Peter, James, and John. The vision on Patmos was not for everybody, but it was indubitably true for John, when he was in the Spirit, and in the solitude upon his lonely isle. "If the vision tarry," said the prophet Habbakuk, "wait for it; it will come and it will not be late." Have we lost the art of waiting? Are we so busy and preoccupied that even fifteen additional minutes is too long to wait while others commune with their Lord? Must persecution come to the church, or tragedy, or sickness pin us to our beds before we let our souls catch up with our bodies?

> Around us rolls the ceaseless tide
> Of business, toil and care;
> And scarcely can we turn aside
> For one brief hour of prayer.

We may never see what John saw on Patmos, but we can at least be, as he was, in the Spirit on the Lord's day. We can practice the art of worship. As Dean Inge pointed out—if we spent fifteen hours and fifty-five minutes of the sixteen waking hours of the day looking at and dealing with material things, and only a hasty five minutes over spiritual things, it is little wonder that material things seem two hundred times more real than the things which are unseen but eternal.

One Sunday in an English cathedral town as the vicar and his guest preacher were preparing to go over to the cathedral for Evensong, the heavens opened and a cloudburst descended from the sodden skies. The minister's wife decided to stay home and brew a cup of tea against their return. When they came back, she asked a question that apparently needed no answer. Were many there? "Full, full," said her husband. "Full of the glory of the Lord." God was there, and his angels. As we say in the preface to the Holy Communion, "Therefore with Angels and Archangels and with all the company of heaven, we laud and magnify thy glorious Name; evermore praising thee, and saying: Holy, holy, holy . . . Heaven and earth are full of thy glory." If that has never happened to you, no wonder you find it difficult to understand the psalmist when he cries out with eager anticipation, "I was glad when they said unto me, let us go into the house of the Lord." He was in the Spirit on the Lord's day . . . are you?

If we are not to be like Willy Loman, ignorant of who we are, and having the wrong dreams—all, all wrong—we must practice the presence of God. We must seek his face in prayer and worship, let him find us in the book where the voice which is as the sound of many waters is to be heard.

When the World Conference of Christian Youth was held in Oslo at the close of World War II, the final rally was a worship service at which the fiery and indomitable Bishop Berggrav was the preacher. At the time the cathedral was undergoing extensive renovation, and the scaffolding surmounted by a plank floor completely obscured the ceiling. Up yonder, where they could not now see him, the Bishop said, a renowned artist was painting a mural which would depict the Kingdom, the power and glory of Christ.

But as yet, nothing of all this could be seen. They would have to return when the scaffolding was at last taken away, and the hidden glories would be revealed.

This is a perfect parable of Christ's hidden reign in our world. "We see not yet all things put under Him, but we see Jesus . . . !" And with the eyes of faith we behold

> . . . through all this fleshly dress
> Bright shoots of everlastingness.

# THE SECRET OF GREATNESS

"But so shall it not be among you: but whosoever will be great among you, shall be your minister: and whosoever of you will be chiefest, shall be servant of all"—Mark 10:43-44.

STRANGE ISN'T it how few people have ever been called great so that the title really stuck? People are like mountains. Often you have to get away some distance before you can estimate their true size. Perspective gives you insight. As long as you are in the midst of the mountains you can't tell a foothill from a peak, but when you get far enough away, the foothills shrink to their true size, and the mountains grow taller and taller. Then there's no mistaking which is a Matterhorn or a Pike's Peak. They stand forth in sunny outline, brave and clear against the blue of heaven. So it is with men too.

Take a man like Mr. A. He was in politics most of his life, and politics then were no nicer than they are now. In the confusion of his day he seemed such a mole-hill of a man that these are a few of the names his contemporaries called him: "Weak, unfit, an imbecile, criminal, the tool of lawlessness, a perjured wretch, a felon and a traitor." Who could such an infamous wretch be? Hitler? Stalin? Benedict Arnold? Guess again. It was Abraham Lincoln! Such he may have seemed to those who were his contemporaries, particularly his critics and his enemies. But in the perspective of the years he grows taller and taller. We would be inclined to agree with the judgment of the poet who likened him to a mighty oak in the forest that in its fall left a vast and vacant place against the sky.

That must be the reason why so few people have the title "the great" thrust upon them. There are so few giants among men. When I tried to set down on paper a list of the names of those who have been called great in order to see if there were some common denominator in their greatness, I could think of only four men in history who have been called great—Frederick the Great, Peter the Great, Charlemagne, and Alexander the Great. So far as I can see, about the only things they had in common were that they sat on thrones, wore crowns, and were mighty men of war. But sitting on a throne and wearing a crown is no guarantee of greatness, and crowns have somewhat gone out of style nowadays, being found oftener in museums than upon heads. What made a man like Alexander, for example, justly deserve the title "the Great"?

For one thing, he believed in himself. He believed that he was descended from heroic stock, that the blood of great men ran in his veins. He was brought up on Homer, and carried that heroic book with him on campaign. He cut the Gordian knot—a man of action and quick decision. He became the first world conqueror whose kingdom stretched from shore to shore, from the Mediterranean to the Indian Ocean. When he died in Babylon at the age of thirty-three, he could indeed weep because there were no more worlds to conquer. He had literally "marched his armies off the map." They had no idea where they were.

Well, Alexander stands for a certain idea of greatness. Greatness consists in getting to the top of the heap. Greatness means being able to throw your weight around, to overcome your enemies and become monarch of all you survey. Yet the sorry record is that greatness like that may be good as long as it lasts, but it doesn't last very long. Alexander's kingdom didn't outlast Alexander! When he was buried, so the record runs, his hands were made to protrude from his gorgeous casket to show that he brought nothing into the world, and was taking nothing out of it. He was all unkinged. Before his death when one of his generals asked him to whom all his power should go, he replied with a riddle: "To the strongest." So his kingdom fell into four pieces, a piece to each general. Lest his widow and child dispute the division, one of the generals saw to it that Alexander's widow and infant son were murdered.

It has not escaped attention that both Jesus and Alexander died at the age of thirty-three. And each of them represents a different idea of greatness.

"Jesus and Alexander died at thirty-three
One lived and died for self; one one died for you and me.
The Greek died on a throne; the Jew died on a cross;
One's life a triumph seemed; the other's but a loss.
One led vast armies forth; the other walked alone.
One shed a whole world's blood; the other gave his own.
One won the world in life and lost it all in death;
The other lost his life to win the whole world's faith.

Jesus and Alexander died at thirty-three.
One died in Babylon; and one on Calvary.
One gained all for self; and one himself he gave.
One conquered every throne; the other every grave.
The one made himself God; the God made himself less;
The one lived but to blast; the other but to bless.

When died the Greek, forever fell his throne of swords;
But Jesus died to live forever Lord of lords.

Jesus and Alexander died at thirty-three.
The Greek made all men slaves; the Jew made all men free.
One built a throne on blood; the other built on love.
The one was born of earth; the other from above.
The one won all this earth, to lose all earth and heaven;
The other gave up all, that all to him be given.
The Greek forever died; the Jew forever lives.
He loses all who gets; he wins all things who gives.[13]

How does Jesus answer our question? Let him now finish
the sentence with which we began: "Whosoever will be
great among you, shall be your minister; and whosoever of
you will be the chiefest, shall be servant of all."

It was a sad disappointment to James and John to discover that the place of honor which they coveted—one to
sit on the right hand and the other on the left hand in the
Kingdom of God—was not a patronage plum to be handed
out to political favorites. It was a shock to be told that they
would have to revise their thinking and find greatness not
in eminence, not in being top man on the pyramid, but in
humble, lowly service. "Even the Son of man came not to be
ministered unto, but to minister."

Service, then, is the first secret of greatness. Whenever
men have been called great, there has been this common
denominator of service. Napoleon was a conqueror too, but
no one ever called him great, because he served no cause,
only himself. But a man like Alexander (to call him to the
stand once more) was not wholly selfish. He not only

marched his men off the map—he changed the map. He changed the thinking of the world. He was born at a time when democracy meant the rule of the *demos*, the people, but the unit of democracy was the tiny city-state. The horizons of a man's world were the walls of his own little town. Alexander changed all that. He made men citizens of the world. He served his own generation.

Jesus served not only his own generation but all men. "Ye know that they which are accounted to rule over the Gentiles exercise lordship over them; and their great ones exercise authority upon them. But so shall it not be among you." The red badge of service is the hallmark of Christian royalty.

And the idea has spread. Service clubs, as you know, started out to be anything but service clubs. Their escutcheon was a knife and fork rampant on a field of snowy white tablecloth! After initial success they began to languish until someone discovered that only service is a motive big enough to keep the breath of life in these noonday organizations. "Whosoever will be great among you shall be servant of all."

Yes, the idea has spread until even those who do not pretend to be orthodox Christians have caught on too. Here is George Bernard Shaw talking sense for once: "I am of the opinion that my life belongs to the whole community, and as long as I live, it is my privilege to do for it whatsoever I can. I want to be thoroughly used up when I die, for the harder I work, the more I live. I rejoice in life for its own sake. Life is no 'brief candle' for me. It is a splendid torch which I have got hold of for a moment, and I want to make it burn as brightly as possible before handing it on to future generations."[14] Well spoken, George Bernard Shaw!

Well, which do we choose: the disciples' seat of honor or Jesus' way of humble service? Just what in the last week have you done for Jesus' sake? You got paid for the hours you worked so you don't expect thanks for that. What have you done? What service have you rendered beyond the call of duty? We must take our place with those who want to be served, or those who serve. Shall it be James and John, or Jesus, ministered unto or ministering?

Once again, the secret of greatness is to be found not only in service in His name, and for His sake. There must be more, Jesus says. Greatness is to be found in sensitiveness as well. In answer to James and John's request, Jesus replied, "Ye know not what ye ask: can ye drink of the cup that I drink of, and be baptized with the baptism that I am baptized with?" What was this "cup," this "baptism"? Was it not the cup about which our Lord prayed in the garden, the cup of bitter suffering which he drank to the bitter dregs? Was it not the bloody baptism of the Cross?

Can we drink of that cup? Can we take at least a sip of the cup of bitterness of which there is so much in our world so that others will have less to drink of that bitter potion? Can we remember in our prayers the homeless, the hungry, the sick, our brethren in the faith behind the Iron Curtain, all of those who suffer persecution for His Name's sake? If we are to be great in the kingdom, in the eyes of Christ—it must be at the cost of sensitiveness to a whole world of need, spiritual as well as physical, which we must do all we can to diminish, by taking to ourselves a part of it.

Now notice a wonderful touch in Mark's narrative. When Jesus asks James and John if they are able, they reply glibly —"we can." Jesus overlooks their ignorance, their blithe assumption of ability, and takes them at their word. "Christ," said George MacDonald, "is easy to please, but hard to satisfy." They have much to learn, but the best of all teachers.

Yet there is more to greatness. The full measure of greatness is to be found in self-sacrifice. "The Son of man came not to be ministered unto, but to minister, and to give his life a ransom for many." In ancient warfare it was the custom to surrender many soldiers as a means of ransoming some high officer. Ordinary soldiers were expendable, and the word for "ransom" is the one that our Lord uses concerning his own sacrifice, a payment of many lives for one. Only Jesus reversed it—he gave his one life as a ransom for many.

In a private room in a great city hospital a patient lay fighting for his life. He had fought all his life, hard but not always fairly and not always clean. The sign on the door said, "No Visitors." At one side of the bed stood the doctor, and on the other side the special nurse. But a Visitor had come into the room, ignoring the sign. This Visitor didn't believe in signs. He watched while the physician gazed at the hands which had been used to taking much but giving little. He saw the doctor adjust the stethoscope and listen to the faint beat of the heart, and saw him shake his head. Then the Visitor bent low and asked the dying man, "Would you like to go back and try again?"

To go back and live selfishly is finally to lose life. But to live today and tomorrow in the spirit of service, in sensitive awareness and in glad self-sacrifice is to find the secret of deathless greatness. Wouldn't you like to go back and try again? The Lord of life himself invites you to go.

# SONS OF ONE FATHER

"For this my son was dead, and is alive again; he was lost, and is found. And they began to be merry"—Luke 15:24.

BACK IN the year 1920, in a little Esthonian settlement not far from the Russian border, some children were playing in the village street. The youngest was a child of three, named Michael. When you are three, you have to do what the older children say, or there is trouble. Well, Michael decided to run away from his playmates and hide in the woods. He thought they would miss him soon and come looking for him. But when they didn't, and it began to get dark and cold (for it was March, and the snow still lay deep in the woods) Michael started out for home. Only he had wandered so far into the woods that he could not see the clearing where the road ran, so he couldn't find his way. Soon it was pitch dark in the woods. He was cold, and hungry, and tired, and frightened—and lost.

Several hours later two soldiers driving a supply wagon heard the boy's cries in the woods, picked him up and took him to the city, and left him at an orphanage. There they put him to bed at once with a high fever, a very sick child, suffering from exposure. For weeks Michael's life hung in the balance, hovering between life and death, then the balance slowly slipped in the direction of life. He was just skin and bones by that time, but that didn't matter now that he could eat. The worst was that he had completely lost his memory. If they asked, "What's your name?" he answered, "I don't know." "What's your father's name?" "I don't know." "What do they call your elder brother?" "I don't know." The answer was always the same, "I don't know." So they called him Michael Nesnajew, because Nesnajew means "Don't know" in Russian.

One day a kind lady came to the orphanage in search of a foster child. When she heard about Michael, she chose him right away and took him home with her. The years passed. When Michael had finished school and was ready to go to the university, they wouldn't enroll him without a birth certificate. And of course he had none. So they took the proper steps. It was just a formality, the police explained, but they must insert an ad in the newspapers of the district, asking if anyone might possibly know the names of the parents of a child who had been lost about sixteen years before, who was then about three years old. They should report to the police.

Several days later a farmer came to the station and asked if he could see Michael. He looked searchingly at the young man, and turned his head to one side as though to say, "It could be he." Then he asked Michael to take off his jacket and roll up the left shirt sleeve. There, on the upper arm was a large scar. "It's my boy," cried the farmer. "See, there's where a horse bit him when he was two years old."

What followed is beyond words to describe, but we can imagine his joy and wonder and amazement. Like the father of the prodigal he could say, "This my son was dead, and he is alive again; he was lost and is found." And they began to be merry. (Luke 15:24)

When they had first missed him that March day, they had searched the woods all night, but found no trace of him. But through all these years his father and mother had kept alive

44322

the hope that somehow, somewhere, by a miracle, he might be alive and would come back. Now here he was. Home again. This was where he belonged. Even his foster mother, much as she loved him, couldn't begrudge him this. To think of it—all these years he had been so near his own home, and still he didn't know where he lived, didn't really know his father or mother.

Perhaps this true story can provide us with a frame through which we can look at another story, one which we know very well indeed—the parable of the prodigal son.

There was a man, says Jesus, who had two sons; and the younger of them said to his father, "Father, give me the share of property that falls to me." and the father divided his living between them. Not many days later, the younger son gathered all he had and took his journey into a far country, and there he squandered his property in loose living.

Looking at the parable through the framework of our modern story, you notice at once certain resemblances and certain striking differences. Both the three-year-old and the other son left home. Both got lost. But you would pity the former and blame the latter, and the reason is that the three-year-old was not responsible, while the other deliberately made a prodigal of himself.

But the deliberate prodigal was a prodigal even before he went into the far country. The sin of the prodigal did not begin the moment he began to waste his inheritance and sow his wild oats. It began much earlier at home, with the demand for his exclusive use of the property for his own selfish purposes. Even before that it sprang from the evil desire to break off the relationship of father and son, to renounce the fellowship of the home, to withdraw his obedience to the father's will in the life of the family.

The far country, someone has said, is one which can be reached without making a journey, because its boundaries are located within the human heart. The prodigal's motto is "give me." That spirit, the spirit of selfishness and exploitation is found not only in the dives and night clubs of the far country, but in much more refined places. Indeed as one commentator points out, "If we were asked for an analysis of the greatest disruptive force in society today, could we answer better than by saying that, in some shape or other, we are all, individuals, classes, nations and races, making the demand made by this youth: 'Give me my share of the property.' "[15]

The second observation that we make is this: just as the three-year-old found, so did the prodigal find that it is a cold, cold world, and that instead of finding happiness in his freedom he found misery, instead of joy there was grief, plenty soon turned into want. As Robert Burns wrote out of his bitter experience,

> The best laid schemes o' mice an' men
>     Gang aft a-gley,
> An' lea'e us nought but grief an' pain
>     For promised joy.

The prodigal has his "fun" as he called it, only to discover that there is a difference between fun and joy, and his kind of fun brought sorrow and sickness and surfeit and self-loathing. Then suddenly he came to the end of his resources. His money ran out, and he began to feel the pinch. He had complained that his father took too much of an interest in his affairs when he was still home. Now he discovered that when you are down on your luck and alone in a great city, people pass you by as if you were a lamp post. Jesus said once that the devil was the father of lies, and from Adam in the garden of Eden, to the prodigal son in the far country, to the present hour there is no greater lie than this—"Go ahead and indulge, you want to have fun don't you?"

The third observation is that, thank God, the prodigal reached the turning point before it was too late. "He came to himself," Jesus says. He thought things through. The three-year-old didn't know his name, or who his father was, but the prodigal son did know. He realized his folly. "How many hired servants of my father have bread enough and to spare, and I perish with hunger. I will arise and go to my father, and will say unto him, Father I have sinned against heaven, and before thee, and am no more worthy to be called thy son: make me as one of thy hired servants." He came to realize that after all there was no place like home, no friend as true as his father, no lasting joy save in the life of obedience, self-discipline, and service.

If all this is so, why did the father allow the son to go away in the first place? We come here upon the mystery of man's freedom. In God's creation apart from man there is law and order, unwavering obedience to God's laws of nature. Only when you reach the level of man is there freedom—freedom to say "Yes" or "No." If God wanted puppets as the crown of creation he would have provided us with leading strings by which he might move our heads and hands and feet. But he doesn't want puppets. He wants people. He wants loving children who freely and willingly choose his way and his will. But freedom to do right must mean freedom to go wrong as well. Obedience involves the possibility of disobedience. God pays us the compliment of singling us out for liberty. He lets us go because he must allow us to choose freely.

But along with this liberty that cannot, that will not, keep the prodigal home against his will, there is also at the same time a love that will not let him go. The father waits with eager impatience. Aristotle might say that no gentleman would be guilty of running in public, but the father of the prodigal unashamedly runs to meet him. He comes half way. Like the father of the three-year-old, he hopes and never gives up hoping that some day his lost lad would find the homeward way.

"The heart of the eternal" as Jesus portrays it unforgettably here "is most wonderfully kind." The returning prodigal asked only for justice, and got mercy. He asked for another chance, to start out as a slave, and was reinstated as a son. From now on his goodness would be a genuine response, not a grudging obedience. Love so amazing, so divine, demands his soul, his life, his all.

> If when I had turned me from the ways of sin
> And sought my home, my lot had been to find
> My father justly wroth, no longer kind;
> If to my prayer the answer stern had been:
> "Thou sayest well, 'Unworthy' enter in,
> But take a servant's place, a son no more;
> 'Tis only mercy openeth the door,
> That thou the bread of servants mayest win";
> Then might I fancy, while my tasks I wrought,

Somewhat I earned of Him, and somewhat paid
Of all my debt, on this my pride had stayed.
But now the robe, the ring, the joyous feast!
Ah, the greeting kiss, the Father's breast!
My pride is lost, o'erwhelmed in love unthought.

If only the story ended there it would indeed be the grandest story ever told. But to call it the prodigal son is to misname the story, for it is a story of *two* sons, both of them prodigal. The younger son broke all the commandments as far as sins of the flesh are concerned, but the elder brother was guilty of sins of the spirit, which, because they lay below the surface were much more serious, were perhaps even more deadly, because in the end the younger son was at home, while the elder brother, who stayed at home all his life, was outside in the darkness and, in the words of Jesus, "he would not go in."

His anger, his jealousy, his contempt for the prodigal clothes itself in words of stinging anger, "This your son who has devoured your living with harlots." He has no way of knowing this for sure. At best it is only a guess, and at worst hearsay, but it reveals the puny size of his soul. Love, says Paul, is quick to believe the best, but the elder brother is quick to believe the worst. Kipling suggests that maybe the elder brother bore a share of responsibility for his younger brother's leaving home. Certainly he didn't make things very pleasant around the house when he was there, and he obviously didn't get very much fun out of his religion. There is an idea abroad among moral people, says Stevenson, "that they should make their neighbors good. One person I have to make good: myself. But my duty to my neighbor is much more nearly expressed by saying that I have to make him happy, if I may." That was not the elder brother's sentiment at all, but I believe our Lord would have approved.

Whom did Jesus have in mind when he sketched this unattractive son? The Pharisees? Probably. But not them alone. A scholar said to his friend, "I've discovered the identity of the elder brother." Who was he? "Myself." He who discovers his own place in this picture is on his way to discovering the heart of the gospel.

> And more and more it may be thou shalt see,
> Upon life's loom how thread to thread is bound:
> None for himself, but man and fellow man,
> Or near or far, meet on one common ground,
> Sons of one Father since the world began.[16]

But now, in this closing moment, let your glance fall where Jesus meant it to fall—on the central figure, the father who waits for and pleads with his sons. Michael Nesnajew's father waited for sixteen years, but this Father is waiting still, after all these centuries. Where are you in this story? Sick of home, like the prodigal was at first; self-sufficient, as he started out; homesick, as he became; or home, where he belonged?

# WHEN YOUR CUP RUNS OVER

MY TEXT today is a page torn from the war diary of King David. Often in his troubled career David had to lay aside the scepter for the sword, and the royal purple for the royal armor. By the strange fortunes of war he now found himself "tenting on the old camp ground." His tent was pitched near Bethlehem—the very spot where he had often played as a child. In these same hills where he now stalked the enemy he had long ago tended his father's sheep. Under the same sycomore where he now rested, he had often laid down in green pastures. Yonder, a mile or so away in Bethlehem, so well remembered, were the still waters of a tree shaded well.

Unaware that anyone was listening, he talks to himself: "Oh, that one would give me water to drink of the well of Bethlehem, which is by the gate."

Three mighty warriors swing
Their shields in place, for he who cried is king,
Beneath whose chariot wheel fenced cities fell;
They vanish where Philistia's bowmen swell,
But he heeds not, in thirsting for the spring
That holds no taste of tears, whose waters sing
Sweeter than trumpets of all Israel.

Forgotten are the things he valued most;
Strong rock-walled Zion, fortress of his land
Grows dim before green pastures polled with rain—

Far from the black tents of battling host
Ruddy as dawn he moves with harp in hand,
A shepherd dreaming on the hills again.[17]

But the next moment he wakens from his reverie. What had these three warriors done? They had broken through the enemy lines. They had walked boldly up to the well beside the gates of Bethlehem. Filling the canteen with water, they had raced back to safety before the Philistines could fit arrows to their bows and send a futile rain of missiles after them. There they stood before him with their gift for which they had gone in jeopardy of their lives. Sometimes I'm sure that David was the worst scoundrel in scripture, but here he showed himself every inch a king. For a long time he held that brimming cup of water in his hands, while great tears welled up in his eyes and rolled down his cheeks. When he found his voice at last, he whispered, "Is not this the blood of the men that went in jeopardy of their lives."

This little incident from the wars of David provides illumination and instruction for life today. Consider this first—in the midst of war's tribulation it gave David cause for thanksgiving. This is in no way to justify war, or to try to glamorize it. War is a nasty business. It is not glamorous or glorious. A veteran pointed out that war is attractive only to those who have not had first-hand experience of it. This is corroborated by the statement of the modern general who called it "Dirty, dull, dangerous, and expensive." Cicero, a good many years ago, concluded that the worst peace was better than the most just war. This is too sweeping a generalization, but one for which there is considerable supporting evidence.

War, the product, may be uniformly bad but, when we consider some of its by-products, we do find some fleeting good when we see courage such as these three men showed in risking their lives out of loyalty and devotion to their commanding officer. War appeals to the basest impulses in man. It brings out his worst side. It can also, upon occasion, bring out that which is best in him. Certainly this is no specious plea for having wars so that men may prove their valor and determination, any more than a man would advocate arson because it brings out the heroic best in firemen who risk their lives to save the victims of fire.

It seems to me, however, that a principle is illustrated that is of broad significance. "There is a soul of goodness in things evil would men observingly distil it out," said Shakespeare. I talked once with a father whose boy was one of the finest lads I have ever been privileged to know. He had lost his boy in the war, and there were wounds in his heart that time would never heal. Yet he paid his own boy this tribute, "Joe was always one to think of the other fellow first. And I don't suppose we should begrudge him this, if he gave his life for somebody else." Tribulation has a way of bringing not only the worst but also the best to the surface. Joe was a GI who went in jeopardy of his life, and never came back.

Life is poorer for his having gone, but his self-sacrifice is like a brimming cup held to grateful lips to drink.

As you look about do you not see cheering examples of a like spirit? Think of the people you know who are good soldiers bringing refreshment to other lives even though their particular battlefield may not be the bloody field of war, but some spiritual field of struggle, or some handicap over which they have triumphed and brought inspiration to others.

The pastor of a church in one of the large cities of this country had for several years battled with a disease that finally robbed him of his sight. His congregation gallantly refused to consider his resignation. But how could a sightless pastor manage to carry on the manifold activities of a city parish? His council, then his congregation became his eyes. Their cars were placed at his disposal, so that laymen and pastor called arm in arm on the sick, visited the homes of the parish, did the work of an evangelist. As one put it, "He lost two eyes and gained six hundred!" So a congregation was drawn into closer fellowship because of trouble. The fires of tribulation refined his spirit. People who might have been unimpressed and unmoved were now stirred to the very depths by a man who discerned spiritual truth more clearly than ever before. A man and a congregation that refused to accept defeat as final have shown how cause for thanksgiving can be brought forth out of tribulation.

Those three men before David with the draught of water from Bethlehem's well stand as a perpetual reminder of an understanding of life that is opposed to the attitude of multitudes of people in our day. These men conceived of their duty in life as providing, at whatever risk, the waters of refreshment for others to drink. Others seek the satisfactions of life in taking, in accumulating, in squeezing out of life as much as they can get. Why will we not learn that it is not in getting that we receive life's satisfactions? Why will we not believe our Lord's saying "It is more blessed to give than to receive"? Where do we stand in this picture—on the giving or on the receiving end?

We have noted two contrasts emerging from this old story: out of tribulation often comes cause for thanksgiving; the deepest joy of life consists in giving not in receiving.

Now as we read on in the story, we are told that when David perceived what these three brave warriors had done, he would not drink the water they had brought in jeopardy of their lives, *but poured it out, unto the Lord*. Their sacrifice became a sacrament. In this human act David caught a glimpse of the real presence of God himself!

We touch here, with reverent hands, the central mystery of the Christian faith. We live in a sacramental universe. Thomas Carlyle pondered this mystery once when he spoke of seeing soldiers being sabered into crows' meat for the sake of a bit of bunting that could be purchased for a few *groschen* at any marketplace. But Carlyle knew well that a flag was not solely bunting and not simply so much goods, but home and history and traditions and attachment to one's native land. It means, "I love thy rocks and rills, thy woods and templed hills." A flag is all that and more—it is the outward and visible symbol of an inward thing called patriotism.

On World Communion Sunday in the great majority of the two hundred and thirty-one thousand churches of our land, men and women of all the Christian communions will gather at the Lord's Table to receive the Sacrament. The mind staggers as it tries to envision the multitude of people in nearly every land of the earth who will be gathering to receive the Sacrament in chapels and cathedrals, in crossroads churches and in metropolitan centers.

Our understanding of the *how* of the sacrament may differ, but not our understanding of the *what*. We may differ as to the mode, but not as to the fact that God himself comes to us in this gift of his love. In that sense at least we are one and can sing:

> The Church's one foundation
> Is Jesus Christ her Lord;
> She is his new creation
> By water and the word.
>
> One holy Name she blesses,
> Partakes one holy food,
> And to one hope she presses,
> With every grace endued.

Whatever Bethlehem meant to David, with its well by the wall, it means immeasurably more to us. For there at Bethlehem God gave mankind a well to satisfy the deepest longing of the human soul, man's never-sated thirst for God.

In that great story, *Wind, Sand and Stars* the French aviator who had himself been forced down in the desert and knew from experience the meaning of thirst, tells of a party of Arabs who visited a tremendous waterfall in the French Alps. Used to the scant brackish waters of the desert oasis, bitter with alkali, they could scarcely believe their eyes. They could not look their fill, and they could not drink enough of the cold, sweet water. After awhile their guide tried to get them to leave, but they would not stir. They waited for the end, for the moment when God would repent of such prodigal madness. But the guide assured these men of the desert, "That water has been running for a thousand years." [18]

For nearly two thousand years this Christ of ours has

offered to men the cup of the New Testament. "If any man thirst, let him come to me and drink." He offers them never failing refreshment, forgiveness, assurance. Let us come then —humbly, gratefully—"My cup runneth over. Surely goodness and mercy shall follow me all the days of my life!" Amen.

# ON DOING NEXT BEST

"A certain man made a great supper, and bade many: and sent his servant at supper time to say to them that were bidden, Come; for all things are now ready"—Luke 14:16-17.

IT WAS Oscar Wilde (if memory serves aright) who told of a maiden aunt who once arranged for a magnificent garden party at her new country estate. Every detail had been most carefully planned. A list of the best people to be invited had been drawn up. The gardeners had brought the garden to June perfection. Even the fickle English weather co-operated with sunshine and cloudless skies. There was only one flaw —nobody came! The poor old woman never recovered from the shock of being snubbed. She withdrew from society, became a crochety recluse, and died heartbroken and alone. Only after her death did they discover the reason for the fiasco. She had overlooked one small but exceedingly important detail. In a cubbyhole in her desk they came upon a stack of identical white envelopes, the invitations which she had forgotten to mail!

Today's parable of the great supper is likewise a story of a great social affair, but one in which that tragic mistake had not been made. The invitations were personally delivered. In Luke's version of the parable the master of the feast made doubly sure by sending his servant around a second time to remind the invited guests and to say that everything now being ready, they should come at once. But nobody who was invited came! Strangely, the invitation which they had already accepted, was now rejected. We need not pause to consider the excuses, which were flimsy enough in all conscience. The point of the parable is not to show up the devious ways of the human mind, to remind us that the human heart, as Jeremiah said of old, "is deceitful above all things, and desperately wicked: who can understand it?" The point of the parable is not man's evasiveness but God's resourcefulness. He did what was next best. He had invited the best people, and they would have none of it. That was just too bad—for them.

He had no intention of going off and weeping in a corner, of becoming a recluse, or even of spoiling a good dinner. If the good people couldn't or wouldn't come, then he would settle for those who were not so good. If the first invited were too busy, or too preoccupied, then he would turn to those who had time hanging on their hands. If the city folk asked to be excused, then what was wrong with the folk of the byways and hedges? He knew what he wanted. He wanted a full house. And he got it.

The first thing I would like to point out on the basis of our parable is that this has ever been God's way—the way of the next best. When he made man he decided to make him with freedom to choose and respond, not a manikin or a marionette to move only when someone jerked the strings. But freedom to choose also means freedom to refuse. The ability to say "Yes" logically involves the possibility of saying "No." Freedom to do right must also mean the option of doing wrong. In the story of Adam and Eve there unfolds for the first time the tragic rejection of God's invitation. God offered man fellowship on terms of man's acceptance of His will. But man rejected the invitation, and so from the very beginning of history God had to do what was next best. The long story of redemption, as recorded in the Bible, is the story of God's resourcefulness in meeting man's stubborn waywardness.

Leap across the centuries to God's next great beginning when Jesus Christ came to live among men. He came with the message of the servant in the parable, "Come for all things are now ready," but the gracious invitation was snubbed by the very people who should have welcomed it, the Pharisees who were specialists in holiness, and the priests who were experts in knowing the will of God. But they would not come. With one accord they too began to make excuse. "This man eateth with publicans and sinners." "He hath a devil" and other excuses a little more polite, but all adding up to the same response—"No, thank you. Excuse me. Sorry. I can't come." It was Paul who awakened the early church to realize the fact that the church had no alternative but to do what was next best and turn to the Gentile world with the invitation of the gospel. And lo, the next best, in the providence of God became actually the better choice, for it meant that Christianity instead of being just a small Jewish sect, confined to an out-of-the-way corner of the Roman world, became a universal religion, the hope of all the world.

Again, signs are not lacking that what God may be about in the twentieth century is the same second choice. The so-called Christian nations have become preoccupied with such material concerns as claimed priority in the minds of the invited guests in the parable: material prosperity, security and economic imperialism, the pursuit of pleasure and luxury, the preoccupation with sex that is so much a part of modern life and living. It all adds up to a polite refusal of God's invitation—"I pray thee have me excused." Nations that have been traditionally Christian for more than a thousand years and now present the spectacle of empty churches and apathetic congregations need not wonder when, as at recent ecumenical meetings, the swarthy men from the lanes and hedges—from mission lands—come forward to assume the places of leadership that have gone by default. If Germany, or England, or Italy, or Scandinavia, or America reject the invitation to God's feast and fellowship, then that is too bad—for them. God will go out into what we might think of as the byways and hedges of the world—to New Guinea, or Ethiopia, or India—to find his obedient servants, men who don't mind being next-best guests in the banquet hall of God's fellowship. His house will be full. If we reject his invitation he will go somewhere else.

There is a corollary to this truth on the human plane—doing what is next best. It often turns out in the end to be better than expected even in the first instance. One shining example will suffice. Back in 1723 the townsfolk of Leipzig in Saxony were gravely disappointed by the refusal of their number-one candidate to accept the post of cantor at St. Thomas Church, where for three centuries a tradition of good music had made a shining reputation for the city and its leading church. With ill-concealed chagrin the city fathers announced the appointment of one J. S. Bach as cantor, with the spiteful comment, "That he had been chosen, since no better candidate was presently available." The "better candidate" who had disappointed them was a

second-rate musician whom you can identify today provided
you have a large enough musical dictionary to look up his
name, but the man who was chosen as next best has his music
sung today by a thousand school choirs, and in ten thousand
churches, played on millions of radios, records, and pro-
grams! Bach at least was under no illusion about the terms
of his election, and so devoted himself to showing in the
only way he could that they had indeed made no mistake.
It is no crime to be second choice—the crime is in being content to be second-rate when you have the chance to be something better.

But let us revert now to the main theme of our parable.
We have spoken of the divine willingness to take what was
next best when the first invited guests refused the invitation
of the gospel. That involves, on the human side, the shame-
fulness of human perversity in being preoccupied with
secondary things, so that God is compelled in turn to do
what is next best. What a sad commentary that is on human
nature and the things that claim our time, our efforts, our
attention, and our selves. Suddenly this old parable comes
alive and becomes entirely contemporary when we realize
that these are the very things that claim priority in our time
and attention. "I have bought a piece of ground, and I must
needs go and see it. . . . I have bought five yoke of oxen,
and I go to prove them. . . . I have married a wife, and
therefore I cannot come." In these three excuses we find
both a summary and a symbol of the things which are often
given highest priorities in the secular life of today: "a piece
of ground"—property; "five yoke of oxen"—horsepower or
atomic power would be the preferred symbol today; "a

wife"—the whole gamut of sex from "the eternal feminine" to its cheapest and most sordid expression.

But, "thou shalt have no other gods before me"—so it stands in the scripture. Business is not godless, but if God is deliberately left out of it, it becomes a devil's booth where all things are sold, each ounce of dross costs its ounce of gold. Do you remember how old Jacob Scrooge awoke to this dire fact in his Christmas Eve dream of the ghosts of things past, when his old business partner appeared to him from the other world, driven with a restlessness that would not let him linger long anywhere. "But you were always a good man of business, Jacob," faltered Scrooge, who now began to think and apply the ghostly revelation to himself. "Business!" cried the Ghost, wringing its hands again. "Mankind was my business. The common welfare was my business; charity, mercy, forbearance, and benevolence, were all my business. The dealings of my trade were but a drop of water in the comprehensive ocean of my business!"

Is that what Jesus meant when he said, "But seek first his kingdom and his righteousness, and all these things shall be yours as well"?

Again the excuse is offered, "I have married a wife, and therefore I cannot come." Yet what is left of marriage, if the most important cohesive and sustaining factor, religion, is left out?

As I entered the church one Sunday afternoon, I heard the phone ringing—urgently it seemed to me. A distraught voice at the other end was calling from the hospital. His six-year-old daughter was in critical condition, and the doctors had told them bluntly she wouldn't live—unless. The father explained that the family had no affiliation, but now when they were at their wits' end, they had just taken the phone book and had gone down the list of churches until they got an answer. When I got to the hospital the father thrust a Bible into my hands (he had gotten it from the church across the street from the hospital). "Tell me where to look for help," he pled. If we could only reach every young couple entering marriage and plead with them to make room for God, for his church, for personal faith, for the family altar in the home. What a satisfaction it was to be able to minister to that family in their need, and what an unforgettable moment it was to look up, as we sat together long past midnight in the hospital lobby and see the nurse standing there and read on her face the miracle, "Thy child liveth!"

Alas, that business should crowd out our Father's business, or that earthly love should crowd out "love divine all loves excelling"—that the things which are next best in life should so often take the place of that which is best of all.

So the parable comes home to our hearts. God is a God who calls. Have we heard the invitation? Have we heeded it? Or have we procrastinated, or been preoccupied? Is our religion just a duty, a drudgery, a bargain that we try to keep? How could this be, when Jesus likens it to the joyful wedding feast of a king's son? How can we make the most joyful religion in the world a dull and juiceless thing, weight rather than wings, a summons that must be kept rather than an invitation which is a delight to accept.

> Jesus, thou Joy of loving hearts,
> Thou Fount of life, thou Light of men,
> From the best bliss that earth imparts
> We turn unfilled to thee again.

We taste thee, O thou living Bread
And long to feast upon thee still;
We drink of thee, the Fountain-head,
And thirst of thee our souls to fill.

Come, for all things are now ready.

# THE PRISONER OF THE LORD

## (*Youth Sunday*)

"I therefore, the prisoner of the Lord . . ."—Ephesians 4:1.

THERE IS an old story about a blacksmith who lived in the Middle Ages, and who in the pride of his craft set his own special trademark on everything he made. When the town he lived in was captured by an enemy force he was one of the first to be arrested and cast into prison. In those days the smith was one of the most important persons in the community. Not only did he shoe the farmer's horses, and make and repair and sharpen the plowshares, he was also the artisan who made swords and spears and shields and all the implements of war. So he was put into the castle dungeon, and chained to the wall. But this did not worry him overly much. As a hard laborer he had tremendous strength. He knew that in every chain somewhere there was a weak link, and when he found that, it would be a simple thing to break his shackles. But as he felt the chain link by link he came upon his own secret trademark, and knew alas that his case was most desperate. There were no weak links in chains he forged. What a tragedy to be held a prisoner by a chain he had himself made.

That old story is well worth pondering today. It has a sharp modern thrust. For how many a man has learned in bitterness that the fetters he wears, which he is unable to break, are the fetters he has forged for himself. As the familiar proverb has it: "Sow a thought and reap a deed, sow a deed and reap a habit, sow a habit and reap a character, sow a character and reap a destiny." Each of these is like the successive links which forge a life and a destiny.

This morning, on Youth Sunday, I'd like to think of three kinds of bondage—the freedom which leads to a bondage which is ignoble, the bondage which leads to a freedom which is noble, and a bondage unto Christ of which Paul testifies, which strangely and wonderfully sets a man free.

There is a liberty which, when followed, leads straight to bondage. The jails of this country are full of men, and in some cases women, who never learned to pronounce the syllable, "No." No one was going to tell them they couldn't do what they wanted to, so inevitably the time came when for self-protection society had to put them under forcible restraint. A chaplain, visiting such a place was passing through the garment factory and saw a prisoner sitting cross-legged, sewing a burlap covering on a bale of overalls. He greeted the prisoner, and said, "Sewing, eh?" "No, chaplain," he replied with a wry smile, "Reaping." He that sows unrestricted liberty forges a bondage not to be broken.

The restraint may not be as drastic as that: As a young man Oscar Wilde decided that there would be no pleasure that he would not taste, no experience in life that he would deny himself—but the end of that daring experiment with life was not particularly happy, and he himself sums up the tragedy of it in these sad words:

> To drift with every passion till my soul
> Is a stringed lute on which all winds can play,
> Is it for this that I have given away
> Mine ancient wisdom, and austere control?

Surely there was a time I might have trod
The sunlit heights, and from life's dissonance
Struck one clear chord to reach the ears of God;
Is that time dead? Lo! with a little rod
I did but touch the honey of romance—
And must I lose a soul's inheritance?[19]

The answer was "Yes"—he had thrown his life away. He had never learned how to say "No" to himself, to curb his desires, to resist temptation, not to follow every whim. So he lost his liberty in a bondage of a very real and permanent sort.

Oscar Wilde reminds us that youth is the peculiar and particular time of life when the meaning of liberty and its limits need to be inculcated in the growing adolescent mind. It is then that the young need to try their fledgling wings. If they are constantly clipped, constantly curtailed in their freedom, it will maim their later years. But on the other hand, if they are not clipped at all, there will be even more trouble ahead. Recently the National Congress of Parents and Teachers published a sprightly handbook for parents of teen-agers, from which I quote a few sentences.

"He's growing, so . . . Decisions handed down by you, his parents, no longer suit him at all. He feels safer, stronger, better making up his own mind about things. He's struggling for elbow room to make decisions, to develop responsibility and his own inner controls.

"He's growing, so . . . He feels the pull ever-present in the adolescent's life. The pull between wanting desperately to be grown up, and at the same time wanting to be sure that his parents are there when he needs them. Being told to 'act his age' sometimes, and 'you're too young for that' at other times, further compounds his confusion.

"He's growing, so . . . He turns to friends of his own age rather than to his parents with his problems and concerns. There's comfort in being with others like yourself when you're living in a world halfway between childhood and adulthood, and you aren't sure just where you fit in.

"He's growing, so . . . At times he needs some restrictions that will protect him and make it easier for him to say no to his crowd. He needs acceptance—as he is . . . He needs to be on his own enough to experience making his own decisions and mistakes. But he also needs guidance enough so that the mistakes he makes are not the kind to hurt others or himself."[20]

It requires special grace to be a youth; it requires a special measure of grace to be a wise and understanding parent also. Every parent should learn to pray daily for the wisdom to know when to hold and curb their children and when to set them free. It is all too easy to use liberty in such a way that it only forges chains of bondage from which we can no longer free ourselves.

Going one step further, we observe that on the other side is the positive and emancipating fact that only where there is bondage of self-discipline does life lead into the finest kind of liberty. This is a truth which is widely despised in our day. C. E. Montague has an essay in which he discusses our modern impatience with the fine disciplines which are necessary before great art can emerge. He speaks scathingly of poems without rhyme or rhythm, pictures which are mere sketches on which modern artists are content to bestow only a "lick and a promise." And then one thinks of the great artists, a Stevenson "playing the sedulous ape" writing and rewriting, comparing and improving, or of a Carl Sandburg who confesses to having rewritten one poem twenty times before he was satisfied, of an Albrecht Dürer who sketched so carefully in making preliminary studies for an altar picture that the famous sketch of the "Praying Hands" has become a masterpiece in its own right. A renowned Victorian artist asked by a lady how she might learn to draw perfect circles as he did freehand and apparently without effort, was told, "All you need to do, madam, is to practice drawing twenty-thousand circles, and you will do it as well as I." The liberty of the artist, the poet, the writer comes at the price of laborious self-discipline.

The same is true of every other worthy achievement—no bonds, no liberty; no shackles, no achievement. It is true even in the matter of human survival. Kipling has a story of an Eskimo boy living in the arctic, being taken on his first sealing expedition. With a wall made of snow to keep off the biting polar winds, he sits at the hole in the ice which his dog has located as a likely place for the seal to appear. There he sits motionless, harpoon in hand, for hours, just waiting for the quick-eared seal to come up for air. To keep his feet from twitching in the long watches, he has tied his legs together by what the hunters call a *tutareang*. This will enable him to remain perfectly motionless. Success or failure hangs upon this willing submission to constraint. It is one of the disciplines of liberty and even of life itself for the Eskimo.

I have no doubt that when Joseph, the young and handsome slave in Potiphar's house, was approached by his mistress to gratify her desire, she undoubtedly used all the persuasions that have ever been used—that no one would know, don't be old fashioned, etc., etc. Joseph was appalled and horrified. He had a master who trusted him, and he dared not be unfaithful to that trust. And there was a higher trust—what God expected of him. He resisted the temptation with these words: "How then can I do this great wickedness, and sin against God?" It was Joseph the slave who was really free, and his master's wife who was in bondage to her own lust. Because she had never learned to take "No" for an answer she was miserable, unhappy, and a lost woman.

With that, we have come to the heart of the matter. You and I were made for freedom, a freedom which grows out of a voluntary bondage. The highest freedom is not that which is bound to something, but to some One. Paul had caught the secret in the words of our text, "I therefore, the prisoner of the Lord beseech you. . ."

In Shakespeare's *King Lear*, Edward (in disguise) joins himself to the discredited king. Lear, surprised that a stranger should want to serve him, asks, "Sir, do you know me?" To which the reply is made, "No, sir; but you have that in your countenance which I would fain call Master." Countless men have found that in Christ—that which they would also fain call Master. Finding him, they have found freedom to live a life that is good and true and pure and satisfying.

So George Matheson cries out for us all—

Make me a captive, Lord, and then I shall be free;
Force me to render up my sword, and I shall conqueror
  be.

My heart is weak and poor until it master find;
It has no spring of action sure, it varies with the wind.
It cannot freely move till thou hast wrought its chain;
Enslave it with thy matchless love, and deathless it shall
    reign.

One of the high tasks which Christ considered it his mission to perform was that of setting men free. "He has anointed me to . . . set at liberty those who are oppressed," he said that day in the Nazareth synagogue as he read from the scripture. By binding men to him, he delivered them from the bondage to those things, those circumstances which had previously held them as in shackles.

Mark Twain tells in one of his books how the Mississippi River cut through a narrow neck of land one night, so that a negro slave who went to sleep in Missouri woke up to find that the land he lived on was now east of the river. Since that made it part of Illinois, it also made him a free man.

The same sort of thing happens to anyone who turns to Christ as his deliverer. He awakens to the same familiar earth, the same people, the same self. Yet everything is wonderfully different, because he stands up as a free man. "If any man be in Christ, he is a new creature: old things are passed away; behold, all things are become new." To the slave of vicious habit, Christ says, "Neither do I condemn thee: go, and sin no more." He breaks the power of the chains of sin, and he sets the prisoner free. To the man who is in bondage to fear, Hebrews teaches, He has delivered them " . . . who through fear of death were all their lifetime subject to bondage."

A little child had been given a small mirror, on the back

of which was a picture of the head of Christ. Fascinated, the child kept turning the mirror over and over. Then, this little three-year-old said something wise beyond her years. "Daddy, me can't see Jesus when me look at myself." No, we can't see ourselves, can't be self-centered (which is the meaning of being lost) when we keep our eyes on him. "Make me a captive, Lord, and then I shall be free." Amen.

# LOVE SO AMAZING

"Beareth all things, believeth all things, hopeth all things, endureth all things"—I Corinthians 13:7.

WE SOMETIMES hear people say, "Well, I can take it," about a grim experience that has befallen them in life. It sounds brave, and it is brave. But it is not the truly Christian response. A Christian doesn't simply try to take it, but to transform it—whatever that "it" may be.

Yonder is an oyster lying placidly on the floor of the sea. A grain of sand, swept along by the tides, becomes embedded in the oyster's soft and sensitive tissues. At first it tries to rid itself of that irritating foreign body. When this proves impossible, instead of getting merely irritated or frustrated, or muttering in oyster-language, "I can take it," the oyster does something creative about it instead. It turns an irritation into an iridescent pearl of great price. That, on the lowly level of the mollusk, is the Christian response.

In today's gospel (Luke 18:31-43) we find Jesus inviting his disciples to go up to Jerusalem with him. There was nothing particularly exciting about that. They had gone to Jerusalem with him many times before. But this time it was different. He knew, somehow, that he was going for the last time. The storm clouds which hung threateningly low upon the horizon, rumbling now and then and flashing forked tongues of lightning, would at long last break in fury upon his defenseless head. For him the end of the road would be Calvary, and the awful cross—that ultimate expression of man's inhumanity. But in going to the cross, Jesus would not simply "endure" the cross. He would not simply take it—he would transform that cross, until this dreadful instrument of brutality, from which men instinctively turned their faces, would become a sign not of shame but of glory, not of defeat but of triumph, not of despair but of hope. In coming days men would even plant it upon the graves of their beloved dead, as talisman of an undying hope and sign of ultimate triumph. This is the greatest metamorphosis of all.

Our epistle also belongs to this same tradition which turns irritation into shining pearl. In it Paul overcomes the temptation to sing the blues and transposes the sour discords and disharmonies of bickering slaves and half-baked Christians into one of the supreme compositions of the human spirit, this great "Hymn of Praise to Love." Throughout his First Epistle to the Corinthians, Paul had been dealing with problems that vexed the early church, living as it did in a world that was completely, enthusiastically, and brutally pagan. But that situation was further complicated by the fact that the Christians themselves were likewise far from perfect, and as a result they had quickly chosen up sides and split into a half-dozen factions. They were going off the deep end in all sorts of imperfect and unbalanced religious aberrations and perversions. As you read along you marvel how this man Paul found his way, with a kind of sixth sense, avoiding the extremes on all sides, patiently unraveling the problems and giving sound advice. He gave guidance which we can still heed today, since from that day to this, the same problems have persisted—only the clothes that the problems wear have a modern cut to them. Then,

Paul suddenly ceases his careful plodding and takes wings. He stops talking and starts singing. "I will show you a better way," he says.

If you study this thirteenth chapter of I Corinthians you discover that while it is often called a hymn, and shows a progression of thought as though it had three different stanzas, it is not merely a poetic creation in which the form controls and dominates the content.

Rather the spirit of love divine has so seized the heart of Paul that it creates the very rhythm, the choice of words, the measured expression. Someone has called it the life of Jesus, set to music. When Tintoretto tried to paint the sea, he finally threw down his paint brush in despair and said, "One cannot paint the sea—it grows ever bigger." Similarly, one cannot preach a sermon on this thirteenth chapter of I Corinthians—it keeps growing ever bigger. But though we must ever fail, failing we can still try.

Someone has likened this first stanza with its like-sounding recurrent phrases to the movement of the waves of the sea marching in majestic procession toward the shore, mounting, swelling like a towering wall, cresting, then breaking with a roar, and dying away in muffled retreat. "Though I speak with the tongues of men and of angels, and have not love, I am become as sounding brass, or a tinkling cymbal. And though I have the gift of prophecy, and understand all mysteries, and all knowledge; and though I have all faith, so that I could remove mountains, and have not love, I am nothing. And though I bestow all my goods to feed the poor, and though I give my body to be burned, and have not love, it profiteth me nothing."

Here in an astonishingly few words Paul distinguishes be-

tween true and false religion in its outward and visible manifestations. There were silver tongued orators in Paul's day
as there are in ours, men who could perform miracles with
words. But what profit is there in rhetoric without the heart-
beat of love to help and encourage? The gift of prophetic
insight likewise, when divorced from love is idle and futile.
Even faith that moves mountains and charity that goes "all
out" is profitless without Christian content.

A man might go so far even as to give his very life. The
day of martyrdom when a man could be burned at the stake
for his faith was not very far off when Paul wrote these
words. But even this would be an empty gesture, without
love. In T. S. Eliot's dramatic story of the martyrdom of
Thomas á Becket, this is precisely what takes place, when
the fiery monk comes to the realization that in inviting
martyrdom he is doing so not for love of God, but out of
hatred of his own political enemies, and the hope that he
will thus in the end triumph over them. "If I give my body
to be burned and have not love, it profiteth me nothing."

As someone has said, "To call Jesus 'Lord' is orthodoxy;
to call him 'Lord, Lord' is piety; but if those who do so lack
his spirit of love, he will disown them." "I never knew you;
depart from me, you evildoers." Loveless faith and loveless
prophecy account for some of the more tragic pages in the
the Christian story through the ages. It has burned so-called
heretics; it has stultified the sincere quest for truth; it has
often been contentious and embittered; and it has often
issued in the denial of Christian brotherhood to fellow-be-
lievers. Faith minus love equals zero.

Augustine tells somewhere of a presbyter who lived in the
days when a man might be called on to die for his faith. As

he went up to Rome determined to seal his faith with his life's blood, he was met by a fellow-Christian whom he had greatly wronged. The man he had wronged stretched out his hand desiring reconciliation, but the presbyter, who thought he had faith enough to move mountains, would not remove the little molehill of misunderstanding, and turned away the proffered hand. He went on to the place of judgment—and denied his Lord. Because he forsook the immediate duty of forgiving love, his faith collapsed in the hour of trial. Though I speak the Augsburg Confession by heart, and know all mysteries of St. Thomas, though I could recite all the proofs of God, the ontological, cosmological, telelogical, and all the rest—it profiteth me nothing if my faith is not informed by love.

> The night has a thousand eyes,
>     And the day but one;
> Yet the light of the bright world dies
>     With the dying sun.

> The mind has a thousand eyes,
>     And the heart but one;
> Yet the light of a whole life dies
>     When love is done.

Let us go on now to glance at the second stanza of this magnificent hymn. When we try to describe this thing called love we are prone to use descriptive adjectives— tender, passionate, puppy, motherly. But the significant thing about Paul's description here is that he uses not adjectives but verbs. It is love in action, love at work that he describes

—not a feeling of emotion, but a motive, a dynamic thing. He uses fifteen verbs in three short verses. He tells us eight things that love does not do, and frames it with two positive affirmations before and four following.

Listen to Paul: "Love is patient and kind; love is not jealous or boastful; it is not arrogant or rude. Love does not insist on its own way; it is not irritable, or resentful; it does not rejoice at wrong, but rejoices in the right. Love bears all things, believes all things, hopes all things, endures all things." (R.S.V.)

How often we say, "love is blind." But is it not hate which is blind? Love has insight, discernment. W. E. Sangster tells of a reply letter from the complaint department in a large store where the typist made all the difference in the world by striking an "f" instead of a "t" in writing, "we fake an interest in every customer." Love does not fake. It takes a loving interest which simply cannot be counterfeit.

Where there is love you will discover it by her speech and by her silence. Love encourages. Love puts the best construction on actions of others. But love is not sentimentally soft. It can be hard too. It knows how to say No! But it is never moody, never hateful, never chews upon a grievance.

Where love is—you can see it pass by. Love finds the way to the dwelling of the lonely, the shut-in, the bereaved. Love crosses "shadowed thresholds dark with fears." But in so doing walks with quiet tread, seeking not her own, never looking for the spotlight.

Where love is you can tell it by its patient endurance. In Phillips' fine rendition, "Love knows no limit to its endurance, no end to its trust, no fading of its hope: it can outlast anything. It is, in fact, the one thing that still stands when all else has fallen."[21]

No wonder we despair in trying to catch all this upon a canvas of words. It grows ever bigger.

As we turn to the third stanza, Paul adds the finishing touch. Love never ends. We live in a world in which men strive to find the permanent in the midst of the transient, the unchanging in the midst of the changing. There was a king once whose name was Ozymandias. Shelley tells us about him.

> I met a traveller from an antique land
> Who said: 'Two vast and trunkless legs of stone
> Stand in the desert. Near them, on the sand,
> Half sunk, a shattered visage lies, whose frown,
> And wrinkled lip, and sneer of cold command,
> Tell that its sculptor well those passions read
> Which yet survive, stamped on these lifeless things,
> The hand that mocked them and the heart that fed.
> And on the pedestal these words appear—
> "My name is Ozymandias, king of kings:
> Look on my work, ye Mighty, and despair!"
> Nothing beside remains. Round the decay
> Of that colossal wreck, boundless and bare
> The lone and level sands stretch far away.'

That is a parable. In this world of time and space, what lasts? Kingdoms? Dynasties? Monuments of knowledge? Nowadays five years is the life span of a spelling book, and tomorrow's discoveries in physics will bring the advanced textbooks of today to the bonfire.

Faith is a great word in the Bible, but the time is coming, Paul reminds us, when we shall not even need faith. What need of faith in the day when we shall see God and know him even as we are known by him? Even hope will some day vanish when the watchman will need no longer ask, "Will the day come soon?" But we shall always need love, for God is love, and in his kingdom love is the law of the realm.

When Wagner wrote his first opera it was hissed off the stage. Musicians threw up their hands when they saw the impossible score. There wasn't a singer who could sing it, or an orchestra that could play it. But still Wagner wrote in sublime confidence that if he continued to write what was in his heart, there would some day come into being musicians who would play and sing his music, and there would be ears to hear it too.

I'm glad that Paul wrote music here too hard for us to sing or play, but music that haunts and shames, and music too that now and then we hear sung. There was a Singer once who sang it perfectly and divinely, and the music is entitled, The Gospel. As we go up to Jerusalem again this Lent, it is that we might catch a glimpse of this love divine, all love excelling. For this love—deep as heaven—has been offered to men over and over and over again so that, like the foolish, loveless Corinthians, we might be shocked by our lack of love, shamed by the poverty of our love, inspired by his love—to sing the hymn of love divine among the sons of men.

# A NEW COMMANDMENT

"A new commandment I give unto you, That ye love one another; as I have loved you, that ye also love one another. By this shall all men know that ye are my disciples, if ye have love one to another"—John 13:34–35.

IT IS very human to desire something as a matter of general principle only to find that we do not want it at all as a matter of practice. There is the old story of the Irish patriot who represented his country in the British Parliament in the old days when his country was an unhappy and unwilling segment of Great Britain. He had just made an unusually impassioned plea for Irish liberty in Parliament. When he sat down the prime minister himself arose and announced that it was his intention to put in motion the necessary parliamentary procedures to set Ireland free from the yoke of British domination. To his surprise, the patriot leaped to his feet at once protesting that to do such a thing would be a great calamity. It would ruin the country. "But—I thought you wanted freedom." "We do, as a matter of *principle*, but not *now!*"

Well, I wonder whether there are not a good many Christians like that, who want Christianity in principle, indeed they do, but not in practice, at least not just now. Love is wonderful in sermons, but we would be terrified to think of putting it to practice in daily life, except for a very limited sphere of application and operation. "Thou shalt love thy neighbor as thyself." In principle who could quarrel with that? But what do you do practically when your neigh-

bor's boy puts half a bag of sand in your gas tank because
you have asked him not to throw sand out of your children's sand box? How do you go about loving a holdup man
when he invites you at gunpoint to hand over your pocket-
book? Can you love a people who are your nation's bitter
enemies? The dilemma is real. We deal with it in the same
way some of our second-class, underprivileged citizens deal
with the pledge of allegiance to the flag: "One nation, in-
divisible, with liberty and justice for all . . . but me." We
love everybody . . . but him and him and her. Or else we
must keep love enshrined as a principle which, some day,
when everybody becomes Christian, we will *then* put into
practice. Eventually, but *not now*. It would be the ruination
of us!

A second difficulty treads upon the heels of the first. Isn't
it the peculiar nature of love that I bestow my affection
upon certain people to a degree in a way that I cannot care
for others at all? If I were God I could love the children of
some African tribesman with just as much affection as I love
my own family. But I am not God, and my love varies, like
gravity, inversely in proportion to the distance between myself and them. It will be much easier to raise a sum of money
to complete the educational facilities of our church, for our
children and grandchildren and the children of our own
community than it ever would be to erect a chapel for a
Christian congregation in Guntur, India.

Yet, here it stands in the gospel without exception or
qualification: "A new commandment I give unto you, That
ye love one another; as I have loved you, that ye also love
one another. By this shall all men know that ye are my
disciples, if ye have love one to another."

We need to think this thing through. What is love? Christian love—how is it different? What's new about the new commandment? When Jesus spoke these words he gave to love a new dimension—a dimension of depth, that was deeper than anyone had ever thought or felt or loved before.

"The confusing thing about love," points out T. E. Jessop, "is that it is a name for two very different aspects of mental life: sometimes we mean by it a particular sort of emotion, sometimes an attitude which can give rise to any and every sort of emotion. When we say that a mother loves her child, it is the second sense that we have primarily in view; we do not mean that she is always feeling the tender emotion of love (which is as impossible as it is undesirable), but that her whole mind has a certain bias or set with respect to her child. Love as emotion is more or less momentary or spasmodic; it is only love as an attitude that is continuous or lasting. It is because the mother has the attitude of love towards her boy that she feels the emotions, not only of love for him, but also of pride in his good qualities, shame for his bad ones, anxiety when he is in danger, and grief when the danger is realized, gratitude to those who help him, and resentment against anyone who thwarts him or does him injury; and it is because of the same attitude that she not only fondles him but rebukes him and others, seeks or makes opportunities of furthering his welfare, and develops and utilizes on his behalf a degree of ingenuity, initiative, patience, courage, and self-sacrifice which she may show no trace of when that attitude is not called into play."[22] That is why love can be angry; why not only the Lord, but also the good parent chastises those he loves.

Now Jesus takes the profoundest love that we know—
parental love—and deepens it, so that the hymn writer speaks
for all of us when he says,

> No earthly father loves like thee;
>   No mother, e'er so mild,
> Bears and forbears as thou hast done
>   With me, thy sinful child.

Human love, no matter how pure, and how profound is not
unlimited. You can kill affection. The family tie can be
broken. But at the cross we find love so deep that it passes
all understanding. These words of the gospel were spoken
in the upper room. All the deceit and treachery in Judas'
heart, all that he planned to do were known to Jesus. Yet
Jesus dealt lovingly with him. At a word, Judas would have
been felled by Peter's ready sword. But with his heart breaking, Jesus still utters no word of reproach. From the cross,
with all the anguish and agony of the nails, the spear, the
crown of thorns, he still manifests the depths of the divine
love of God and prays, "Father forgive them, for they know
not what they do." O the depth of the love of Jesus.

> How deep is his love? Oh, as deep as man's sinning,
> As low as that uttermost vileness can be;
> In the fathomless gulf of the Father's forsaking
> He died for the world and He died for me.

To the dimension of depth then, Jesus also added a new
dimension of breadth. "A new commandment I give unto
you, That ye love one another; as I have loved you." When
our Lord was crucified, his arms were stretched out upon
the cross, as though forever to remind us that the "love of

God is broader than the measure of man's mind." O the breadth of that love. In its embrace it included a rich man like Joseph of Arimathea, but with the other arm it included the poor widow who cast her all into the temple treasury. It took in the aged Nicodemus, and the rich young ruler, and even the little children whom the disciples thought were too much bother. It took in the sinner as well as the saint, the foreigner as well as the native. He was color blind, and race unconscious.

A legend of the war years tells how the pastor of a German congregation was handed a notice as he went into the pulpit during the period when the Nazis were exterminating the Jews. He read, "All those who had a Jewish father or grandfather are herewith ordered to leave this church." There was dead silence, then a few agonized sobs as those Jewish-Christians who had received their death warrant arose and left. "Now," he continued, "all those who had a Jewish mother, or grandmother will also leave the church." In the tense silence, there was a moment of waiting, and then a curious sound of rending wood as though nails were being drawn. The Corpus of the crucifix hanging over the altar was seen to come down from the cross and leave the church before the horror-struck gaze of those who were left. "Narrow," "bigoted," "prejudiced" belong to the words "Christian" and "church" as little as "cold" belongs to "fire," or "darkness" belongs to "light." "God so loved the world (not the Caucasian, Semitic, Mongolian, or any other race, but the *world*) that he gave his only begotten Son, that *whosoever* believeth in him should not perish, but have everlasting life."

At its best the church has always known this and practiced

an all-inclusive love. About the year 200 a lawyer by the name of Tertullian wrote a defense of Christianity addressed to the Roman senate—a hard-hitting apology which still exists. He proceeded to defend the Christians against the slurs and innuendos which had been made against them, and explained the common worship, the common prayer, the sense of brotherhood which made even their enemies cry out, "See how they love one another." He described how they held all things in common, their wives excepted (a practice about which pagan society had little or no scruple); how the Lord's supper was a feast of love to refresh the necessities of the needy, not an occasion for stuffing the well-fed bodies of gluttons; how they gave money not only for the provision of girls and boys who had neither parents nor provisions left to support them, but for relieving old people worn out in the service of the saints, or those who had suffered by shipwreck, or been condemned to the mines or prisons for the faith of Christ.

How broad is his love? Oh, as broad as man's trespass,
As wide as the need of the world can be;
And yet to the need of one soul it can narrow—
He came to the world and He came to me.

"Charity," someone has pointedly said, "was almost unknown till Christ taught people to be hurt at others' sufferings and to rise up and hurry to their aid." He has sensitized the conscience of mankind so that men no longer can be satisfied with the kind of goodness that is negative rather than positive, passive rather than active. His emphasis was not on abstinence from evil so much as on the energetic pursuit of goodness. Never once did Jesus say "Thou shalt not."

Always it was *thou shalt*. The man he held up as a warning was the rich man in the parable who did nothing wrong, so far as the record goes, but who did nothing right either— he had no eyes for Lazarus at his gate, no ears for the cry of need. To the rich young ruler who protested that he had kept all the commandments from his youth up, he gave a new commandment, "Go and sell all thou hast, and give" because he saw that his goodness was "faultily faultless, icily regular, splendidly null." His example for praise was the Samaritan who could pay only part of the hospital bill at the makeshift hospice of an inn, and promised to pay the rest on his return.

"A new commandment I give unto you, That ye love one another, as I have loved you"—and that is a stretching operation. It may mean refusing the coin to the begger who asks alms, but helping him to overcome his alcoholism. It may mean patience, and wrestling in prayer. It may mean learning with Paul what it means to say, "Beareth all things, believeth all things, hopeth all things, endureth all things. Love never faileth."

But how, you ask, how do you get the power to deepen your love, and broaden it until it becomes more and more inclusive? Jesus himself could never have done it without realizing that in his life and his death, in his sufferings, God was being glorified. This was not only submitting to God's will but co-operating with it. God was strengthening him, sustaining him. "True Christian love is a sacred flower; it springs from the soil beneath the cross moistened with the dying Saviour's blood."

A modern artist has painted a most striking portrayal of the Crucifixion. As you look at the picture at first you see nothing familiar or conventional at all, because most pictures of the Crucifixion are painted from the perspective of the earth, looking from below up to the cross. But this one is painted from above, looking down from above. Suddenly you feel hushed and awed and bowed and strengthened. God the Father is in this too.

How high is his love? It is high as the heavens,
As high as the throne of His glory must be;
And yet from that height he has stooped to redeem us—
He so loved the world and he SO loved me.

"By this shall all men know that ye are my disciples, if ye have love one to another."

# NEW PATCHES AND OLD BOTTLES

"No man also seweth a piece of new cloth on an old garment: else the new piece that filled it up taketh away from the
old, and the rent is made worse. And no man putteth new
wine into old bottles: else the new wine doth burst the bottles,
and the wine is spilled, and the bottles will be marred: but
new wine must be put into new bottles"—Mark 2:21-22.

It is an observation trite but true that most people have
sight but not vision. They don't really see. How many
people had walked in orchards and watched apples fall?
But only a Newton really saw the principle that was involved—the law of gravitation which the falling apple illustrated. How many generations of people had idly watched
the lid of a teakettle on the stove lifted by the force of the
steam generated by the fire beneath? But only a James Watts
really saw what was happening and went on to invent the
steam engine. The faculty of creative imagination—of observation and wonder—is rare; but it need not be as rare as it is.

All this came to mind as I thought of our text for today:
"No man seweth a piece of new cloth on an old garment . . .
no man putteth new wine into old bottles." Where did our
Lord get this observation? Obviously not from the rabbis.
They were so enamoured of the old, addicted to the traditional, bound to the past, that when rumor ran that a new
star was rising out of Nazareth, they were ready to put a
quietus to that with an old proverb, "Can any good thing
come out of Nazareth?"

Where did our Lord get this incisive saying? Did he see his
own mother one day sew a patch on the well-worn cloak

that had grown too small for him, but would do for his younger brother, Joses? Perhaps she discovered after it had gone to the river where the family washing was done that the patch—made of new cloth—had shrunk and torn away the old cloth to which it had been sewn, so making the last estate of that garment worse than the first.

In the village bazaar, surely, he must have seen hanging in the shop after the grape harvest the wineskins which were the poor man's bottles, bulging with the newly-made wine. Undoubtedly he stood and watched, as a boy will, when the old, dry skins had cracked, and beneath on the dirt floor a purple pool had collected. He had heard the wisdom of the marketplace, "For new wine, you need new wineskins."

One day, early in his public ministry the disciples of John the Baptist came to Jesus with a problem—they had observed that Jesus and his disciples did not keep the traditional weekly fasts which had been customary for centuries. Why? To answer that question Jesus really asked another question. Why do people fast at all? The answer was obvious. In Jewish religion, prayer, fasting and almsgiving were religious practices designed to secure God's favor. Fasting was an outward and visible manifestation of an inward state of uncertainty. It was a means of gaining merit in the eyes of God in order to have the assurance of salvation. The Pharisee in the parable put it neatly in a package when he said, "I fast twice in the week, I give tithes of all that I possess." If he did his part, wouldn't it be reasonable to expect that God would do his? *If.* That, however, was the question.

But our Lord's answer starts with another point of view altogether. His disciples were not in a situation of lack and want toward God. They were not busy building a bridge of merit from themselves to God. It was rather God who had himself broken a way through to man. When the bridegroom has come after he has been long expected, then the time has come not to fast, but to feast. "Joy to the world, the Lord has come!" That, Jesus says, is the reason why he and his disciples did not fast.

To be sure, he adds, the day of joy will some day pass. The bridegroom will be taken away. He knew what was in men—that the human heart is deceitful and perverse. But while the bridegroom was present, the watchword was: Rejoice, and again rejoice.

Then in that memorable phrase he turned the question around and asked the disciples of John, "Do men sew a piece of new cloth on an old garment? Do men put new wine in old wineskins?" If they do, the result is a tragedy, a loss, spoilage of cloth and contents alike, an actual dissipation of what under other circumstances would be preserved.

Now, what does all this mean to us? This surely is the abiding and unchanging truth through all the passing generations. If Christ is the bridegroom, can we live as though something new had not been added to life—a new radiance, a new joy, a new spirit, a new power? Christianity is a wedding, not a funeral (and even a funeral is different because we sorrow not as those who have no hope). Yet often it would seem that if someone really wanted to know just what difference Christ had made in our lives, he would have to retain the services of a private detective to discover. These things ought not so to be.

Friedrich Nietzsche was no friend of traditional Christianity, but sometimes to learn the truth you have to ask not your friends but your enemies. What did Nietzsche say?

"They must look more saved—these Christians. They must sing better songs, and look more saved, if I am ever to believe their profession." How true! And why not?

The other day, as I was waiting for the traffic light to change, my attention was drawn to the car approaching from the other direction. As it went by, I noticed that the lady driving was smiling. There was no one else in the car, and obviously she hadn't looked at me. She was just smiling as she drove along. I thought to myself, that attitude ought not be one so rare as to occasion notice and comment. So the rest of the afternoon I tried it myself. I looked at the blue of the sky as the sun broke through the clouds—and smiled. Sitting at the symphony, listening to the bitter-sweetness of Mendelssohn's Scotch Symphony, I smiled—not in acknowledgement of someone's greeting, but just in acknowledgement of the presence of the fleeting beauty of harmony.

In his great narrative poem of the transformation of a prize-fighter—hard-fighting, hard-drinking, real tough character—into a Christian, John Masefield described the difference and the joy which came into Saul Kane's life when he let go, and let Christ come into his heart.

> The bolted door had broken in,
>   I knew that I had done with sin,
> I knew that Christ had given me birth
>   To brother all the sons of earth.[23]

There was a new glitter to life, springtime had returned to touch with glory the cold and wintry earth.

Certainly this feeling that something new has been added, no, that some One transformingly new has been added to life, is what is behind the gospel narrative today. The old Hebrew ritual is an old wineskin which simply cannot contain and confine the strong new wine of the gospel. This certainly is the primary truth which our text wishes to inculcate.

But every scripture passage has subsidiary truths, and one of these is the distinction which must be made between the precious content and the container in which the truth is enshrined. Sometimes men ascribe the same value to that which is meant merely to be the container as they do to the thing contained. For instance:

I love the Lutheran church. I was born into it. My father chose it, became a minister in it, as his father before him and his father's father. But I do not believe that what was the will of God in the sixteenth century, when he raised up Martin Luther to reform the church, is necessarily his will forever. I must not confuse the wineskin with the wine. Indeed we live in days when from the mission field the question is constantly arising concerning the ultimate validity of denominationalism. Must a native of Southern India coming into the fold of Christ through the preaching of a minister of the Presbyterian church—U.S.A. become a Northern Presbyterian? Must a Gold Coast African become a Missouri Lutheran when he doesn't even know where Missouri is? I have no way of knowing what shape, in the providence of God, the church will take. But I do know that the unanswered prayer of our Lord was "That they all may be one, as thou, Father, art in me, and I in thee." New wine needs new wineskins. Anyone with any spiritual discernment must be aware of the spiritual fermentation of our times in the uneasiness of the ecumenical church and the desire to make it more universal—like the pattern of unity in the Godhead itself.

Once again, these two little parables of our Lord are a great source of comfort and confidence as we face the inevitable changes which time makes with the forms of thought. Time makes ancient good uncouth—in religion as elsewhere. Jesus Christ is the same yesterday, today and forever—but the *human* interpretation, the external clothes of thought, the theologies that men have devised, grow old and one day get beyond patching and need to be cast aside. Time was when men, thinking of the atonement, used the crude metaphor of a hook baited with the flesh of Christ. The devil, like a rapacious shark, devoured Christ—only to be caught on the hidden hook, which caused his overthrow. Certainly that way of expressing the central conviction of the Christian faith, our Lord's atoning death on the cross, is not thereby convincingly stated to our generation.

I believe with all my heart that the Bible is the Word of God, but that does not commit me to any particular human theory of inspiration. That God has spoken in his Word, and that he still speaks to us through his Word as he speaks nowhere else on earth, is a precious truth without which I could not be a Christian. Yet when Luther himself said, "The Scriptures are the cradle in which Christ is laid," he was making precisely the distinction which Christ makes in our text—the difference between content and container.

Shall we leave it there today? The distinction which we constantly need to make is between the temporal and the eternal, the container and the contained. Think of the joy which Christ brings when he becomes the inner spring of our life, and think how that joy simply shatters the old forms, the old, wearisome moral striving, the old-time legalistic religion which was never good enough because it lacked the power of God to salvation which Christ brought and brings to those who believe in him.

# WHAT LACK I YET?

## (Confirmation)

WHAT LACK I yet? This question, you will remember, was the one the rich young ruler asked of Jesus (Matt. 19:16-22). He had come with the question about what good thing he should do to inherit eternal life. Jesus' answer was that, if he would enter into life, he should keep the commandments. He named off half a dozen of them, including the summary of the law: "Thou shalt love thy neighbor as thyself." The young man wasn't one to be put off by the obvious. He wanted to know more. He was persistent. He felt that he already had a passing grade in keeping the commandments, and he said, "All these things have I kept from my youth up: what lack I yet?"

Young friends of the confirmation class, today we reach the end of a chapter. For two years we have been studying every week in a concentrated form the Bible and a little book about the Christian faith written four hundred years ago—the *Small Catechism*. Some of you have learned your lesson well. Some of us have done less than our best—although we won't go into that. But each of you might well be asking the same question that the rich young ruler asked, "What lack I yet?"

Well, certainly the church would say to you that we never finish learning about our religion, and we should never stop growing in our faith. In fact we *must* continue to grow or we perish. Life is like flying an airplane. The pilot can't be satisfied just to get up in the air and then coast along. The pull of gravity is so great that he must make sure the propellers are turning properly if he is to reach his destination. So must we keep on the move as Christians. A healthy dissatisfaction with *what* we are and *where* we are is one of the real tests of a growing Christian.

Let us think about that question this morning for a little while—"What lack I yet?" The church's answer is given in the form of a beautiful confirmation prayer for you as you kneel at the altar: "The Father in Heaven, for Jesus' sake, renew and increase in thee the gift of the Holy Ghost, to thy strengthening in faith, to thy growth in grace, to thy patience in suffering, and to the blessed hope of everlasting life."

First of all you need to be *strengthened* in faith. The time will come—indeed it comes very quickly for some young people—when they begin to grow critical of their homes, their parents, their church, and community. Youth is a time of dissatisfaction. Like the young lad in the parable who felt cribbed, cabined, and confined at home, youth dreams of gathering everything together and getting as far away from it all as they can. Away from all the rules and regulations. They want to be their own boss. They don't want to be told they have to do anything. Consequently, when they cut loose, they chuck all the duties and try to enjoy just the privileges. Sometimes they show their independence by stopping coming to church, just as they seem to stay away from home as long and stay out as late as possible.

Moreover before long you'll find people trying to destroy what faith you have. Why—I don't know. But the voices that we hear in the old Bible stories will whisper in *your* ear: "Yea, hath God said?" "If there is a God, why doesn't he make it so you must believe in him?" There will be those who insinuate that religion is an illusion, dope, just a tranquilizing drug to keep you quiet and happy.

Long long ago a very wise man wrote, "A little philosophy inclineth man's mind to atheism, but depth in philosophy bringeth men's minds about to religion." When your faith is put to the test—you may be sure it will be if the devil has anything to say about it—say to yourself: "My faith will be all the stronger for this trial. Which am I going to believe—the doubts of little me, or the magnificent triumphant beliefs of Jesus, of Paul, of Martin Luther? What lack I yet—well it may be that I still need to have my faith in God strengthened, established, settled." For that the church too prays today and will continue to pray for you through the days to come: "The Father in Heaven, for Jesus' sake, renew and increase in thee the gift of the Holy Ghost, to thy strengthening in faith."

Second is "thy growth in grace." Everybody loves a baby. But babyhood is meant to be followed by childhood, and childhood to grow into adolescence, and adolescence to grow into adulthood. Growth is a mark of life. And growth is a mark of the Christian life. Just as we need to have our faith strengthened, so we must also grow in grace. It's what Paul, in another place, calls the fruits of the spirit: love, joy, peace, longsuffering, gentleness, goodness, faith, meekness, temperance.

A little boy asked his mother once—as his mother was measuring how tall he was on his birthday:

"Mother do you still grow?"
I let the measuring rod drop . . .

Do I still grow?
This afternoon I suffered
From unkind words, and yet I smiled:
Last year I would have been proud
To make a sharp reply. This morning I set aside
My own desires to help someone else:
Last year I would have cried, "I will have my way!
Let others yield to me."
Do I still grow?
Yes, child, I think so . . .
But how slow and hard my growing is![24]

Growing up isn't easy, and Christian growth isn't easy either. The apostle tells us in Ephesians that one of the purposes of the church is to help us to grow . . . "Till we all come in the unity of the faith, and of the knowledge of the Son of God, unto a perfect man, unto the measure of the stature of the fulness of Christ: that we henceforth be no more children . . . but speaking the truth in love, may grow up into him in all things."

"What lack I yet?" "Patience in suffering." When you were very small your parents tried to protect you as much as possible from getting hurt. When you reached out your hands for the pretty flames in the fireplace, they rushed to keep you from getting burnt. They put a gate at the top of the stairs, so you wouldn't tumble down. As we learned in the catechism, God does the same for us. He puts a gate at the top of the steps, which we call the Commandments, to keep us from falling into sin and so getting hurt.

But even with the best of care life does hurt us. Little boys fall into wells, children get burned by fire. Pain and suffering is somehow also a part of God's plan, and all of us, sooner or later, in one way or another, need to learn patience in suffering. Many years ago in Avila, Spain, there was a girl named Teresa. She grew up to be a great Christian leader, and founded an order or society. In those days women weren't supposed to go around doing things like that, so she had a good many trials and tribulations. But she never lost her sense of humor, which helped her over many a rough spot. It is said that on a journey in the last year of her life when everything seemed to go wrong, to add insult to injury the burro on which she was riding balked and threw her into a mud puddle. "O Lord," she prayed, "when wilt thou cease to strew our path with obstacles?" Then when he seemed to reply, "Murmur not; for thus it is that I treat my friends," she immediately responded: "Ah, dear Lord, and that is why thou hast so few!" If we can only believe that the suffering, the wounds that we receive in life —when they are not simply the result of our own folly or stupidity—are the "faithful wounds of a Friend," even when they do not seem to be so, then we will gradually learn patience in suffering, and with it grow in grace and be made strong in faith.

Once again—"What lack I yet?" The fourth thing for which the church prays today is that you may have "the blessed hope of everlasting life." One of the things nobody knows is how long he is going to live. The insurance companies can tell us, if there are enough of us, how long we are going to live as a group. Do you know how long you are expected to live according to the life insurance tables? Your expectancy, as the life insurance actuaries put it, is two-thirds of the time between your present age and eighty. For example, if you are fifteen now, the difference between

your present age and eighty is sixty-five. You can expect
to live two-thirds of that time, or another forty-four years.
That seems like a long time—now. But the saddest people in
the world are those who only have time, and not eternity.

A. E. Housman has written some lines that are bitter-
sweet, lovely but pessimistic:

> Loveliest of trees, the cherry now
> Is hung with bloom along the bough,
> And stands about the woodland ride
> Wearing white for Eastertide.
>
> Now, of my threescore years and ten,
> Twenty will not come again,
> And take from seventy springs a score,
> It only leaves me fifty more.
>
> And since to look at things in bloom
> Fifty springs are little room,
> About the woodlands I will go
> To see the cherry hung with snow.[25]

What did Housman lack? He lacked eternity. He did not
know that there is more life where this life came from. He
did not know our Lord who brought life and immortality
to light. But we have threescore years and ten—and then
the blessed hope of everlasting life. How happy we should
be to have all this—and heaven too!

We started with the rich young ruler and his question,
"What lack I yet?" You remember how the Bible story
turned out. Jesus told him to go and sell what he had and
give it to the poor and then come and follow him. It was

a staggering demand. It was a sacrifice so great that he found that he was not prepared to make it. He wanted to keep his money and get eternal life too. The point was that money was his real god. But God is a jealous God who refuses to have any other gods beside him, or before him. The young man would have found real happiness if he had obeyed Jesus' command. But he went away sorrowful, for he had great possessions. Or should we say that his possessions had him?

It is a tragic thing in life that so many go away sorrowful, and break the heart of Jesus, for the poor pleasures, the prizes and privileges that this world holds out instead.

> At the devil's booth all things are sold,
> Each ounce of dross costs its ounce of gold.

But my prayer is for each of you, and others are praying it too, that you will keep your pledged word, by the help of God, until the day when he himself will say, "Come, ye blessed of my Father, inherit the kingdom prepared for you from the foundation of the world."

# CHRIST'S PROMISE TO FAITH

"For verily I say unto you, that whosoever shall say unto this mountain, Be thou removed, and be thou cast into the sea; and shall not doubt in his heart, but shall believe that those things which he saith shall come to pass; he shall have whatsoever he saith."—Mark 11:23.

THERE ARE three ways of saying things, as C. E. Montague has pointed out. "You may state them about twice as big as they are, or about half as big as they are, or if you have skill and complete confidence in your skill, you may state them only just as big as they are."[26]

Now wisdom lies in knowing just when to use each of the three ways of expressing truth. Just now, I take it, most of us are fed up with the gross distortions and exaggerations which seem to be a necessary part of political oratory. But that should not blind us to the fact that there are times when the only effective way of saying a thing is by making it twice as big as it ordinarily seems. When that master of English speech, Shakespeare, wanted to portray the terrifying power of a guilty conscience he used both the overstatement and understatement as a terrible contrast. When remorse has taken hold of Macbeth after murdering the king, and there is blood on his hands, he cries,

Will all great Neptune's ocean wash this blood
Clean from my hand? No, this my hand will rather
The multitudinous seas incarnadine,
Making the green one red.

Lady Macbeth, on the other hand, answers him:

> A little water clears us of this deed.

In sober actuality, we would say that Shakespeare was stretching the facts not a little in both directions. But he was not stretching the *truth*. Remorse turned morbid does feel that way, just as callousness tries to pass off important things as trivial.

So our Lord, when he would impress upon us the tremendous significance of *faith* and its indispensability for life, if life is to be lived creatively—he too put it in unforgettable hyperbole, " . . . whosoever shall say unto this mountain, Be thou removed, and be thou cast into the sea; and shall not doubt in his heart . . . he shall have whatsoever he saith."

Now it is worth noting first of all that Jesus expected us to take this word of his, shall we say, with a grain of salt. He did not mean it literally although he did mean us to take him *seriously*. There are some things in life which even God cannot remove. God cannot be false to himself. No matter how much or how often we say to a falsehood, "Be thou truth," it remains what it is. We have all heard of the fourth grader who closed her prayer with this petition, "And dear God please let Louisville be the capital of Kentucky." Yet not even a child's fervent prayer could move Louisville from its place on the banks of the Ohio River, and set it down in the center of the state where the capital of Kentucky is actually located. As a certain famous evangelist used to say: "If you eat salt herrings, even the grace of God won't keep you from being thirsty." Whatever else Jesus meant by this saying about faith moving mountains, he did not mean that if it were only fervent enough, faith could nullify truths or avoid consequences. God is the author of truth, therefore he will not lie. God is holy, therefore we are bound to be disappointed if we expect some alchemy to turn leaden motives into golden deeds. "Whatsoever a man soweth that shall he also reap."

Nor need we spend much time on another misunderstanding, as though faith were a divine substitute for human action. Before the Civil War a slave, who afterward rose to eminence in American life, said that he had prayed for many years for freedom. Then one night his prayer got out of his head and down into his heels and he ran away from bondage into freedom. The oppressive mountain of human slavery was cast from him.

Having safeguarded this saying of Jesus against the misunderstanding that faith if it is only powerful enough can do without human response in action, or can even fly in the face of truth, let us now ask, what does Jesus mean by "this mountain"? Does he not mean those stubborn facts, the appallingly grim difficulties that beset life like a range of mountains, high and lifted up, impeding progress, over which there does not seem to be any trail or pass? Adam Burnet lists a few of those mountain peaks in the whole range of *personal* problems: "It may be poverty that defies us, (he says) or business cares overwhelm us. It may be what Bunyan calls the 'Hill Difficulty' that slows down a man's brave pace till he is struggling desperately at last on hands and knees. It may be the growing inroads of weakness or disease, or old age, and we cannot see past that black bulk to any prospect of peace or happiness. It may be a great grief that we feel as if

we could never leave behind, as if it will always tower up and
darken the road. Or it may be a great fear, that all the omens
point to as being presently a dead certainty."[27]

Beyond the realm of the mountain-like personal trial and
tribulation there is a further range of religious difficulties.
There is doubt itself, rising up like the Matterhorn to
threatening heights. Bishop Wescott was examining a young
candidate for holy orders once, and he asked him "Have
you any difficulties in religion?" "None, my Lord," con-
fidently replied the embryo curate. "I am so sorry," replied
the bishop. For one who has experienced no difficulties in
faith, there are scores of us who have. Our gospel this morning tells us the cheering story of the nobleman who came
with his prayer to Jesus for the healing of his son. When
Jesus seemingly tried to put him off with the objection,
"Except ye see signs and wonders ye will not believe," the
nobleman overcame that objection with a cry of need which
the Lord could not refuse, "Come down ere my child die."
And his prayer was answered. But scripture tells of another,
David's little lad, just as precious to his father, just as much
prayed for, who was not spared. This mountain too is familiar ground for some here. Or, think if you will of the pre-
vailing secularism of our day and age, of those millions of
our fellow countrymen who "hear their one hope with an
empty wonder, sadly contented with a show of things,"
men and women who have no first-hand acquaintance with
deity, and do not care! Alas!

And beyond the range of the personal, and the religious,
there are the snow-capped ranges, like the Himalayas—such
towering evils as communism, or the ancient, and so far un-

scaled and unconquered mountain wall of war, beyond which the valley of peace seems to lie in impossible remoteness.

Did Jesus mean that we were to say to these mountains, never doubting in our hearts, "Be thou removed, and be thou cast into the sea," and we shall have whatsoever we say? Yes!

Faith can move mountains, because, only faith has the power to "bid eternal truth be present fact." Fosdick quotes a modern phrasing of our thought: "If a thing can be done, experience and skill can do it. If a thing cannot be done, only faith can do it." I think it's worth repeating. "If a thing can be done, experience and skill can do it. If a thing cannot be done, only *faith* can *do* it." We have a saying that seeing is believing. But in a deeper sense it is the opposite which is true, first comes faith then comes sight. First the faith, then the mountain begins to move. When the Panama Canal was first projected, the work was undertaken by a firm of French engineers. But there were almost insuperable difficulties: the enervating tropical heat, the malaria, the heartbreaking landslides. When a cut had been made, the side of the mountain would move, and the work had to be done all over again. Finally in despair the French engineers gave up. Then General Goethals took over. The canal became a reality because he believed, nothing doubting in his heart, and then believing became seeing.

So it is in the triumphs of science—in medical research, for example, where again and again it has proved true, that "if a thing cannot be done, only faith can do it." We might paraphrase those great words in Hebrews not irreverently,

"We see not yet all diseases put under him . . . but we see
. . ." Faith does move mountains.

Again, we say, faith can move mountains because it relies
not upon its own strength, but upon the strength which God
supplies.

> In our own strength can naught be done,
>     Soon were our loss effected;
> But for us fights the Valiant One
>     Whom God Himself elected.

When Morrison went to China as a missionary a hundred
years ago, nearly everybody told him he could never move
that mountain. He said he knew that he could not, but he
knew that God could, and he believed that He would. This
pioneer was a prophet. God had the power, Morrison had
the faith, and that mountain has moved. Now another rival
faith has taken over, and the mountain seems more insur-
mountable than ever before. We need to hear the voice of
Robert Morrison speaking to us from those long-ago days,
"God can!"

What you and I need, what the church needs, what America needs, is a rebirth of faith, the confidence that "whosoever shall say . . . and shall not doubt . . . he shall have."
There is the old story of the barge which was sunk in an
East Coast seaport. Salvaging crews went to work. Cables
were placed under the water-filled barge, and the tugs puffed
away fiercely but ineffectively at the task. Then an engineer brought to the scene huge tanks. These he filled with
water and sank them on either side of the barge at low tide.
Then he pumped out the water after the divers had fastened

the cables from the barge about the empty tanks. "Now what?" they asked. Said the engineer, "Now, we wait." Then the tide turned and as it rose, the tanks floated and began to tug at the wreck. As the tide came up foot by foot, the barge rose with it—lifted by the mighty arms of the sea. All things are possible, said Jesus, to him who believes. If human ingenuity, human devotion, human strength is aided and abetted by the everlasting arms—cannot even mountains be removed and cast hence?

It is said of the father of the sick lad in our gospel, that he believed the word of the Lord, "Thy son liveth." The next day as he neared home, his servants came running with the glad news, "Thy son liveth." He asked them at what time he began to mend, and their answer was, "Yesterday, about the seventh hour the fever left him." We need not only faith, but tokens like that. Blessed is the man who has in his own memory such days and hours. He who has such yesterdays, is not fearful of the morrow. He who knows such mercies, does not fret and he who has a sure word of God, can stand his silence and await the fulfillment of his perfect will.

# THE MAN WHO LEAPED OVER THE WALL

*(Reformation Sunday)*

". . . and by my God have I leaped over a wall."—Psalm 18:29.

IT HAS been many a day since I read so stimulating a book as Monica Baldwin's strange story of convent life entitled *I Leap Over the Wall.* For more than a score of years Miss Baldwin lived behind the walls of a Roman Catholic convent in England, but for ten of those years she was thinking about leaving it under a growing conviction that she had no talent or vocation for that sort of life. The book takes its title from the Baldwin family motto, which is to be our text today. You will find it in the eighteenth Psalm, "For by thee I have run through a troop; and by my God have I leaped over a wall."

Miss Baldwin's leap was figurative, not physical. Her leaving the convent was no furtive flight by night, clambering the high convent walls, but by permission of the authorities, and in the most prosaic fashion imaginable—opening the front door and walking down the steps and out through the gate into a strange new world.

If this were not Reformation Sunday we might be tempted to tarry over the story itself and the intimate glimpses it affords of life behind the walls, a sheltered, regimented, austere life which has not changed appreciably in half a millennium. Easy-going Protestants would be amazed to learn that there are people who actually spend most of their waking hours in the pursuit of holiness—in prayer, in wor-

167

ship, in the deliberate annihilation of personality, in the cultivation of the soul at the expense of the body.

I was amazed to discover that the practice of self-chastisement, the actual lashing of the body with a small whip until the blood runs, while not officially encouraged, is still permitted in such establishments. The same is true of other practices which the psychologist would say pass beyond the realm of normal self-discipline into the shadowy regions of the abnormal and even pathological.

There were light touches too—the wry humor of the dispute in choir over the proper rendition of the Easter gradual which reached such a state that the warring sisters had to take their differences to the Sister Superior for arbitration and settlement! Evidently the devil gets even into such hallowed ground as convent chapels! And there was the pathetic anecdote of the wee mouse mother who brought her latest brood into the world in a corner of the choir stalls, and whose runt ended up in Monica's pocket, so starved was she for companionship.

But we cannot tarry over these details, for more important considerations claim our attention today. This is Reformation Sunday. Today we commemorate another leap over a wall by another fugitive from the monastic life, the Augustinian monk, Martin Luther. His leap and its consequences are of a significance which it is difficult, nay, almost impossible to measure. As a result of that leap, Western Christendom was divided into two great religious communities—those who remained obedient to the Roman hierarchy, and those who became Protestant. The wall of separation, now higher than ever, runs through all subsequent history. It runs through Washington, and through every nation in Europe. It is found in North America and in South America. Tragically it runs even through households in every community of the land, vexing domestic relations and disturbing as nothing else can, the tranquility of otherwise peaceful homes.

What was the nature of that leap over the wall which brought about this great division? Two incidents from Luther's life will make it abundantly clear. Everyone knows that dramatic hour in Luther's career, when he had been summoned before the Imperial Diet where he took his courageous stand, invoking divine assistance, "God help me. Amen." But even more significant were the words that preceded that appeal to heaven: "Unless I am proved to be wrong by the testimony of the Scriptures and by evident reasoning—for I cannot trust the decisions of either popes or councils, since it is plain that they have frequently erred and contradicted one another—I am bound in conscience and held fast in the Word of God. . . . Therefore, I cannot and will not retract anything, for it is neither safe nor salutary to act against one's conscience."

The other scene is less known, but no less dramatic and significant. It took place in Wittenberg itself where Luther had been warned that he was in danger of drastic measures. When the writ of threatened excommunication was placed in his hands, that very night a little band of professors and students gathered outside the town walls and Luther consigned to the flames not only the document which threatened him with exclusion from the Roman Church, but also the books of canon law upon which the despotic authority of the Papacy had been built up (not without recourse to forgery in certain blatant instances) through the centuries.

What did it all mean? Luther never denied that the Church of Rome had a right to be called Christian. He did deny the pope's claim to be Christ's vicar. The wall he leaped over was the wall of religious bureaucracy, a vicious and immoral dictatorship. To his astonishment he found himself not outside the church at all, because he was now standing upon the solid rock of the authority of the Word of God.

Perhaps we can clarify the issue at stake by recalling something that comes as close to us as our own families. When a child is born, he is not yet a person, he is only a candidate for personality. He is a helpless mite of humanity, without freedom, unable to make decisions, completely dependent. The wise parent does not aim at keeping the child always in a state of supine dependence. Some day the child will need to learn to make his own decisions, which involves the right to be wrong. Every true parent aims at making his child not a clinging vine, twining about the parent tree like a parasite, but a tall tree, stalwart, independent.

No fair-minded person will say that the Papacy has been solely a power for evil. But insofar as it has played the part of an oversolicitous parent, building a great edifice of tradition which is accounted superior even to Scripture, it has built walls which eventually had to be surmounted. Luther's tremendous leap, empowered by the gospel, proved once and for all that Rome's claim to exclusive possession of grace and salvation is false.

It was, you may recall, a distinguished Roman Catholic historian, Lord Acton who said that power tends to corrupt, and that absolute power corrupts absolutely. The corrupting power of power such as became concentrated in Rome lay in Rome's unwillingness to recognize any power higher than itself. The curia became a law unto itself. *Roma locuta, causa finita*—when Rome has spoken, that ends it. Even in scientific fields it was not until 1870 that the sun finally received belated permission from Rome to become the center of the solar system. It was a long, long wait from the days of Galileo until that tardy recognition was given.

Why is it that the Catholicism one sees in French Canada or in Colombia, the fiercely bigoted and intolerant Catholicism of Spain and southern Italy is a different sort of Catholicism from the variety encountered in America or in a country like Germany? Is there some connection between the fact that where Catholicism is confronted by a virile Protestantism there you find it at its best? Can there be any relationship between critical observation, intelligent criticism, the need for vigilance, and the quality of religious life that is produced? If so, the best thing that ever happened to Roman Catholicism was Martin Luther! His leap of faith and the train of events that followed compelled Rome to face up to its shortcomings and to clean house with vigor and thoroughness.

The Protestant Reformation then, was from its beginning a religious revolt, in the name of the gospel, against an authority which had turned into an autocracy. With all his heart Luther was persuaded that if a man were entrusted with the gospel and with Christian liberty, he would know or else learn what to do with it. The grave danger that beset Protestantism then and now was and is the danger of misunderstanding liberty. Liberty can be falsely conceived as freedom *from responsibility* rather that freedom *for* responsibility. So vigilance is needed to keep liberty from turning into license. There are disciplines of liberty which we neglect to our peril. We may even get the anomaly of a man claiming to be "a red-hot Protestant"—and still not a member of any church! Many a Protestant who rejoices in having leaped over the wall of repressive constraint has forgotten the apostolic injunction: "Work out your salvation with fear and trembling" and has substituted for it the sentimental and flippant theology of a Voltaire, "God will forgive me. It's his business!"

What is the remedy? Is it a return to Rome? No! "For freedom Christ has set us free; stand fast therefore, and do not submit again to a yoke of slavery." (R.S.V.) If not "Back to Rome," what then? Could it be "Forward to Luther"?

Luther's leap over the wall was not only a leap from a cribbed and too confining authority into Christian liberty, it was also a leap from a narrow and circumscribed ideal of the Christian life to one that was broad as life itself. Here one finds both illumination and insight in reading the pages of Miss Baldwin's book. What pathetic glimpses she gives us of life within convent walls where the pursuit of holiness is life's sole concern. Recall the bodily scourgings till the blood runs, the despising of the body for the salvation of the soul. Remember the little black books in which the sisters try to keep track of their moral progress in a complicated double-entry bookkeeping. Then contrast the joyful evangelical conception of the good life. Do we not have it on our Lord's own authority that it is not good for the man to be alone? Is it not in the family where we come as near as we shall ever come to the kingdom of God on earth?

Luther somewhere tells of questioning a servant girl on her duties. Who had commanded her to work? And the answer came, "My master and my mistress." Again she was asked who had given them the authority, and the answer came that it had come from God. Then, with a happy cry she said, " It is as though I were cooking and sweeping for God himself in heaven!" The good life, in Luther's understanding of it, becomes worldwide—life in the turmoil and stress of the world. "All service ranks the same with God." In the recovery of the doctrine of Christian vocation, we have cause to bless the name and memory of Martin Luther.

As Protestants we should know where we stand. But ere we close let us ask ourselves whether we shall be satisfied to let this wall of separation between Protestant and Catholic stand until the day of judgment. Can the wall be breached? At least let us guard against building spite fences surmounted by the barbed wire of bigotry. There must be a sense in which we can never be happy with walls of separation. Robert Frost cries out "Something there is that doesn't love a wall."[28] While we cannot compromise the gospel, while we cannot pretend that there are no basic differences, we are obliged as Christian brethren to resolve to love even though we may agree to differ. It is a poor Protestantism which by its hatred of Catholicism comes close to forfeiting the spirit of Christ.

Our task, even though we meet rebuff and scorn, is to say what the chaplain on the battlefield said to the dying soldier who refused his ministrations saying, "You don't belong to my church." "But you belong to my God."

This must be our prayer and our hope:

> How fair the Church of Christ shall stand
> A beacon light in all the land,
> When love and faith all hearts inspire,
> And all unite in one desire
> To be as brethren and agree
> To live in peace and unity. Amen.[29]

# NOTES

0. William Law, *A Serious Call to a Holy and Devout Life*. Copyright, 1948, by W. L. Jenkins, the Westminster Press. Used by permission.

1. "There Yet Survived a God" from *Collected Poems of Robert P. Tristram Coffin* (New York: Macmillan Co., 1939).

2. Related by J. Hugh Michael, *The Epistle of Paul to the Philippians*, The Moffatt New Testament Commentary Series (Garden City, New York: Doubleday, Doran, 1929), p. 217.

3. Quoted by Ivan Lee Holt in *The Return of Spring to a Man's Soul* (New York: Harper and Bros., 1934).

4. Mame Wallis, "The Sacrifice of the Will" from *Prayer Poems* by O. V. and Helen Armstrong, (Nashville, Tenn.: Abingdon Press).

5. "The Darkling Thrush" from *Collected Poems of Thomas Hardy* (New York: Macmillan Co.).

6. Laurence Housman, "And the Word Was Made Flesh" from *Masterpieces of Religious Verse* compiled by James Dalton Morrison (New York: Harper and Bros.). Quoted by permission of Sidgwick and Jackson, Ltd., London.

7. "Little Gidding" in *Four Quartets* by T. S. Eliot. (New York: Harcourt, Brace and Co., 1943).

8. Ivan Lee Holt, *The Return of Spring to a Man's Soul* (New York: Harper and Bros., 1934).

9. Related in "The Ballad of the Cross," a poem by Theodosia Garrison.

10. "The House of Christmas" from *The Collected Poems of G. K. Chesterton*. Copyright 1932, by Dodd, Mead and Co., Inc. Reprinted by permission of Dodd, Mead and Co., Inc.

11. Arthur Miller, *Death of a Salesman* (New York: The Viking Press, 1949).

12. "The Retreat" by Henry Vaughan.

13. Charles Ross Weede, author.

14. Quoted in *The Reader's Digest*, July, 1935.

15. Related by J. F. McFadyen in *The Message of the Parables* (New York: Funk and Wagnalls Co.) p. 150.

16. Frances Crosley Hamlet, "But When Ye Pray," from *1000 Quotable Poems*, edited by Thomas Curtis Clark (New York: Harper and Bros.).

17. T. S. Jones, Jr., *Sonnets* (Mosher Press).

18. Antoine de Saint-Exupény, *Wind, Sand and Stars*, 1939.

19. "Helas," 1881.

20. "It's High Time" (pamphlet) (Washington, D. C.: National Education Association, 1955).

21. J. B. Phillips, *Letters to Young Churches*. Copyright 1947, by Macmillan Co. Used by permission.

22. T. E. Jessop, *Law and Love* (London: Epworth Press, 1948).

23. John Masefield, *The Everlasting Mercy*. Copyright 1911, by Macmillan Co. Used by permission.

24. "Growing" by Mary Dickerson Baugham.

25. "Loveliest of Trees" from *Collected Poems of A. E. Housman*. Copyright, 1940, by Henry Holt and Co., Inc. Used by permission of the publisher.

26. C. E. Montague, *A Writer's Notes on his Trade* (London: Chatto and Windus, Ltd.).

27. Adam Burnet in *Church Management*, June, 1935, p. 451.

28. "The Mending Wall" by Robert Frost from *Collected Poems*. Copyright 1930, by Henry Holt and Co., Inc.

29. T. Kingo (1690), "How Fair the Church of Christ shall Stand," translated from the Danish by O. T. Sanden, *The Lutheran Hymnary* (Minneapolis, Minnesota: Augsburg Publishing House).

*Type used in this book*
Body, 10 pt. on 13 and 8 pt. on 10 Janson
Display, Janson
*Paper:* Standard White Antique, G. M. Finish